GUITAR MUSIC OF BRAZIL

THIS PUBLICATION IS NOT AUTHORISED FOR
SALE IN THE UNITED STATES OF AMERICA AND / OR CANADA

WISE PUBLICATIONS

LONDON / NEW YORK / PARIS / SYDNEY / COPENHAGEN / MADRID / TOKYO

Exclusive Distributors:
Music Sales Limited
8/9 Frith Street, London W1D 3JB, England.
Music Sales Pty Limited
120 Rothschild Avenue, Rosebery, NSW 2018, Australia.

Order No. AM968770
ISBN 0-7119-8656-8
This book © Copyright 2000 by Wise Publications.
(Formerly published as Antonio Carlos Jobim For Guitar Tab)

Unauthorised reproduction of any part of this publication by
any means including photocopying is an infringement of copyright.

Edited by Arthur Dick.
Music processed by The Pitts.
Cover design by Michael Bell Design.
Cover photograph courtesy of Tony Stone.
Printed in Malta by Interprint Limited.

Your Guarantee of Quality
As publishers, we strive to produce every book to the highest commercial standards.
The book has been carefully designed to minimise awkward page turns and
to make playing from it a real pleasure.
Throughout, the printing and binding have been planned to ensure a sturdy,
attractive publication which should give years of enjoyment.
If your copy fails to meet our high standards, please inform us and we will gladly replace it.

Music Sales' complete catalogue describes thousands of titles and is available in
full colour sections by subject, direct from Music Sales Limited.
Please state your areas of interest and send a cheque/postal order for £1.50 for postage to:
Music Sales Limited, Newmarket Road, Bury St. Edmunds, Suffolk IP33 3YB, England.

www.musicsales.com

CORCOVADO (QUIET NIGHTS OF QUIET STARS) 6
DESAFINADO (SLIGHTLY OUT OF TUNE) 50
HOW INSENSITIVE (INSENSATEZ) 12
IF YOU NEVER COME TO ME (INUTIL PAISAGEM) 18
MEDITATION (MEDITAÇAO) 24
ONE NOTE SAMBA (SAMBA DE UMA NOTA SO) 32
SOMEWHERE IN THE HILLS (O MORRO NAO TEM VEZ (FAVELA)) 38
THE GIRL FROM IPANEMA (GAROTA DE IPANEMA) 44
WATER TO DRINK (AGUA DE BEBER) 59
WAVE (VOU TE CONTAR) 66
TABLATURE & INSTRUCTIONS EXPLAINED 4

tablature & instructions explained

The tablature stave comprises six lines, each representing a string on the guitar as illustrated.

A number on any of the lines indicates, therefore, the string and fret on which a note should be played.

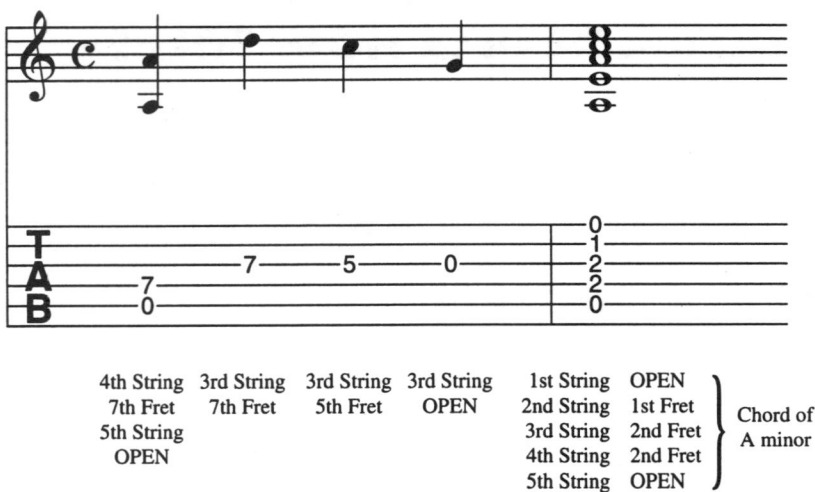

4th String	3rd String	3rd String	3rd String	1st String OPEN	
7th Fret	7th Fret	5th Fret	OPEN	2nd String 1st Fret	Chord of
5th String				3rd String 2nd Fret	A minor
OPEN				4th String 2nd Fret	
				5th String OPEN	

A useful hint to help you read tablature is to cut out small squares of self-adhesive paper and stick them on the upper edge of the guitar neck adjacent to each of the frets, numbering them accordingly. Be careful to use paper that will not damage the finish on your guitar.

Finger Vibrato

Tremolo Arm Vibrato

Glissando

Strike the note, then slide the finger up or down the fretboard as indicated.

Tremolo Strumming

This sign indicates fast up and down stroke strumming.

8va

This sign indicates that the notes are to be played an octave higher than written.

loco

This instruction cancels the above.

This note-head indicates the string is to be totally muted to produce a percussive effect.

P.M. = Palm mute

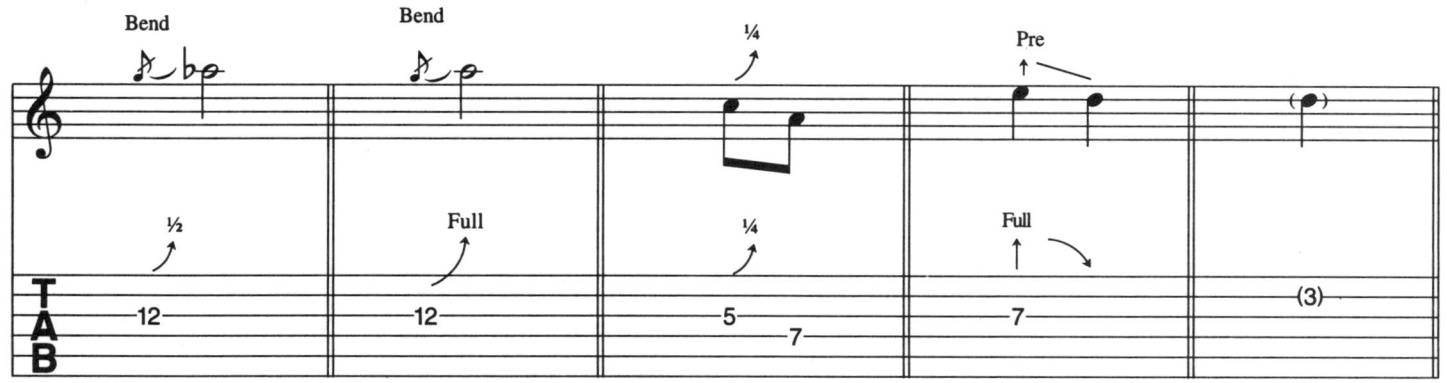

HALF TONE BEND
Play the note G then bend the string so that the pitch rises by a half tone (semi-tone).

FULL TONE BEND

DECORATIVE BEND

PRE-BEND
Bend the string as indicated, strike the string and release.

GHOST NOTE
The note is half sounded

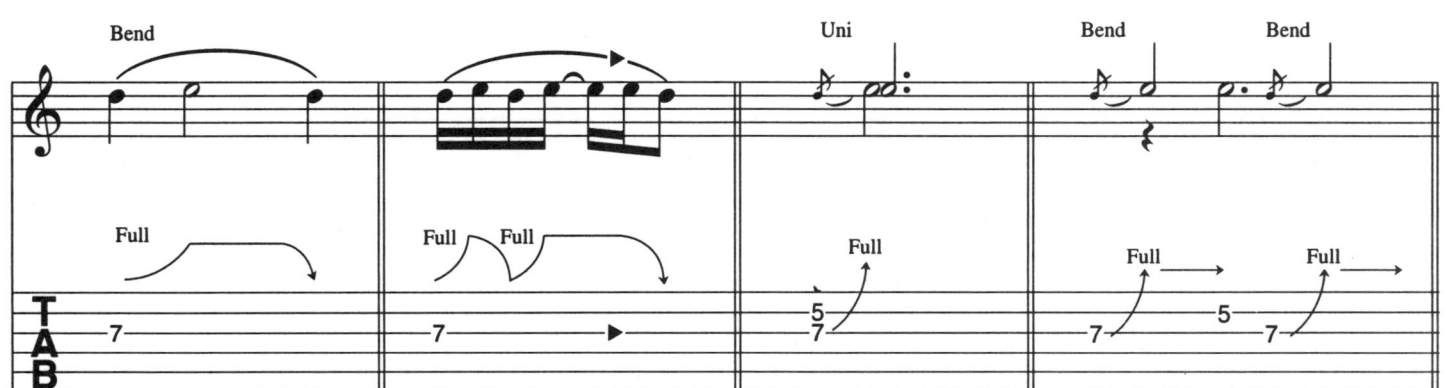

BEND & RELEASE
Strike the string, bend it as indicated, then release the bend whilst it is still sounding.

BEND & RESTRIKE
Strike the string, bend or gliss as indicated, then restrike the string where the symbol occurs.

UNISON BEND
Strike both strings simultaneously then immediately bend the lower string as indicated.

STAGGERED UNISON BEND
Strike the lower string and bend as indicated; whilst it is still sounding strike the higher string.

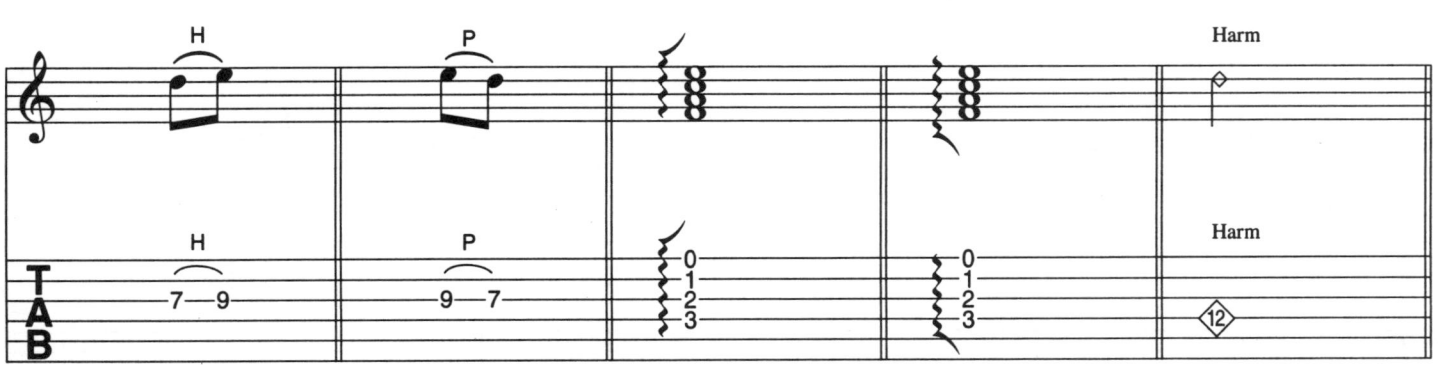

HAMMER-ON
Hammer a finger down on the next note without striking the string again.

PULL-OFF
Pull your finger off the string with a plucking motion to sound the next note without striking the string again.

RAKE-UP
Strum the notes upwards in the manner of an arpeggio.

RAKE-DOWN
Strum the notes downwards in the manner of an arpeggio.

HARMONICS
Strike the string whilst touching it lightly at the fret position shown. Artificial Harmonics, (A.H.), will be described in context.

corcovado
(quiet nights of quiet stars)

english words by gene lees
music & original words by antonio carlos jobim

Corcovado literally means 'hunchback'. It is the name of the mountain overlooking Rio de Janeiro on top of which stands the statue of Christ The Redeemer with its outstretched arms embracing the city below. The music tells the story of a man who lives on the mountain dreaming of a simple life.

© copyright 1962,1965 by antonio carlos jobim, brazil
mca music limited, 77 fulham palace road, london w6 for the british commonwealth (excluding canada & south africa)
all rights reserved
international copyright secured

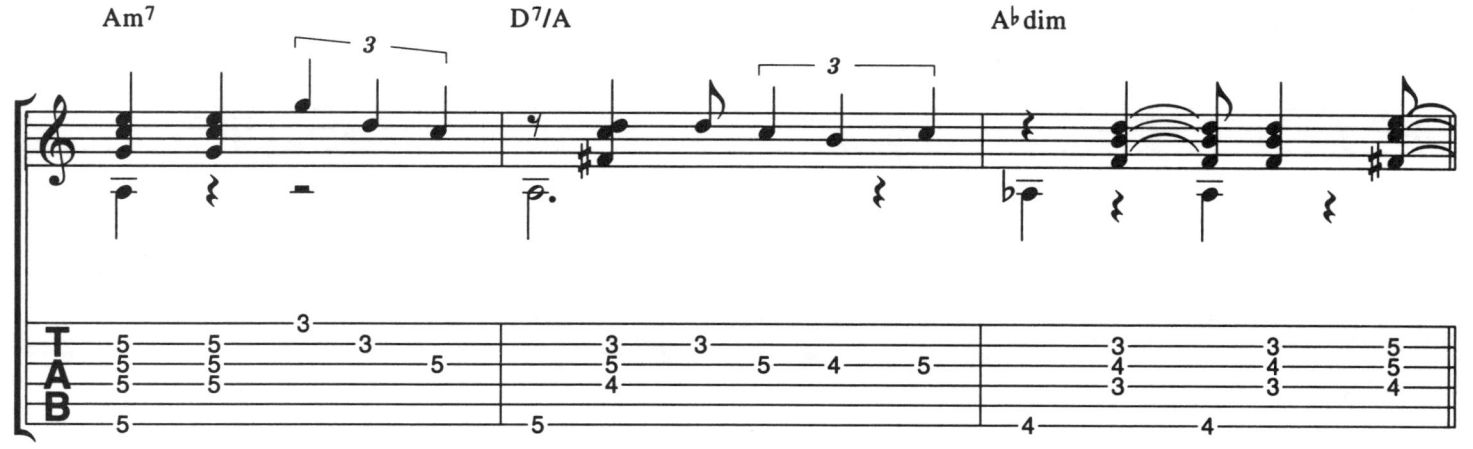
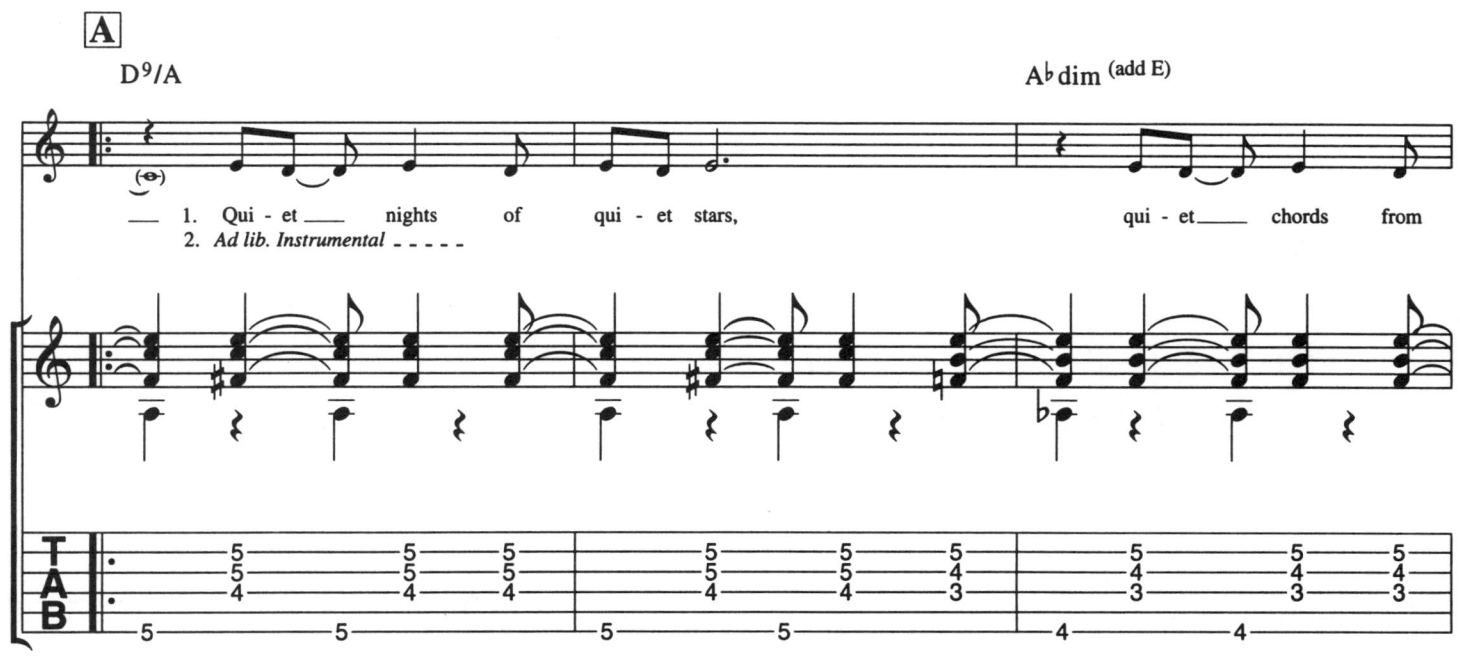
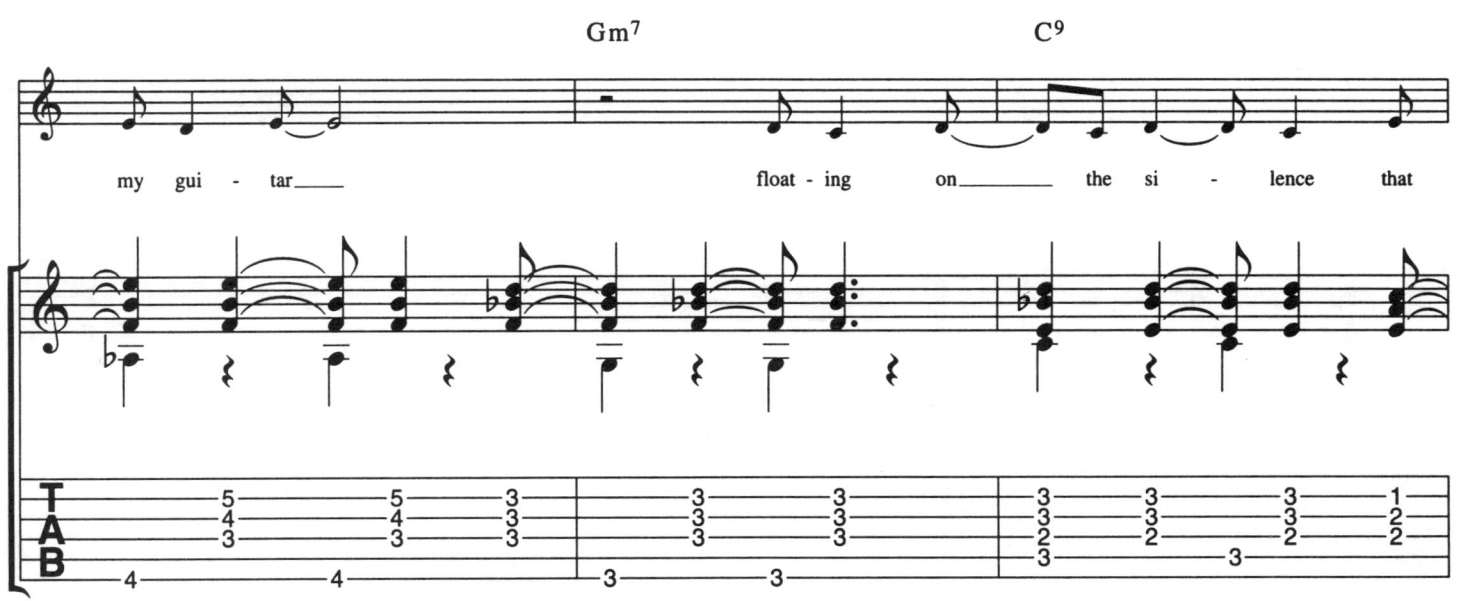

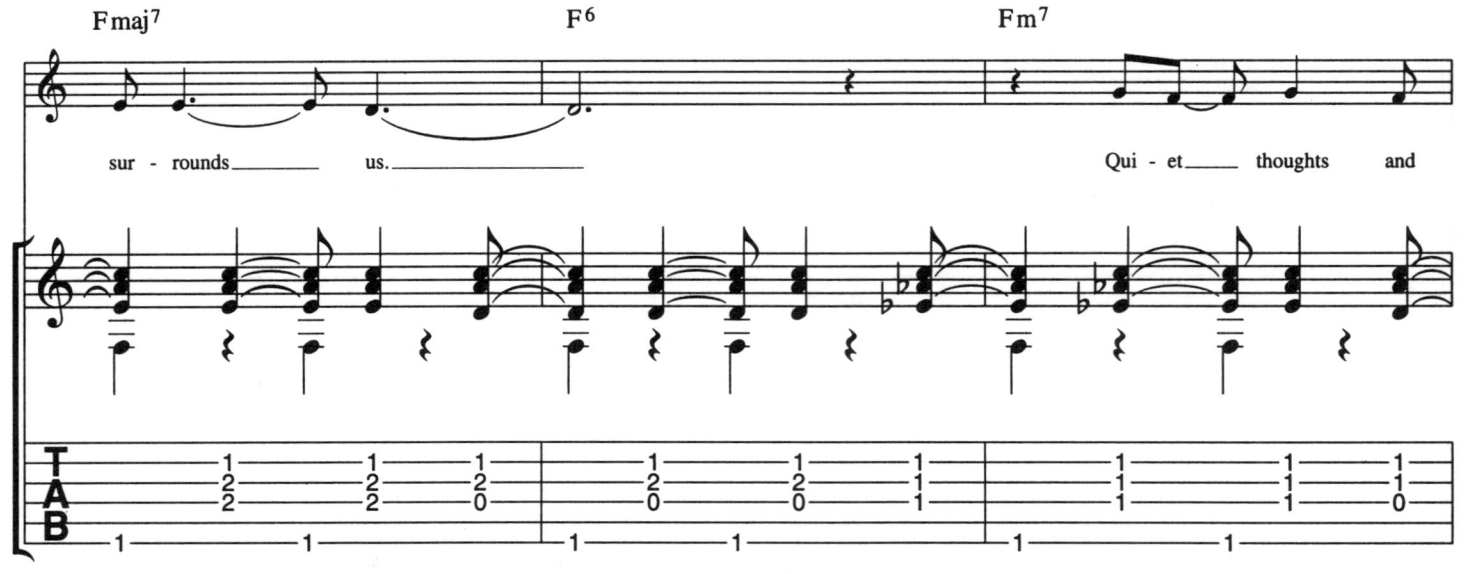
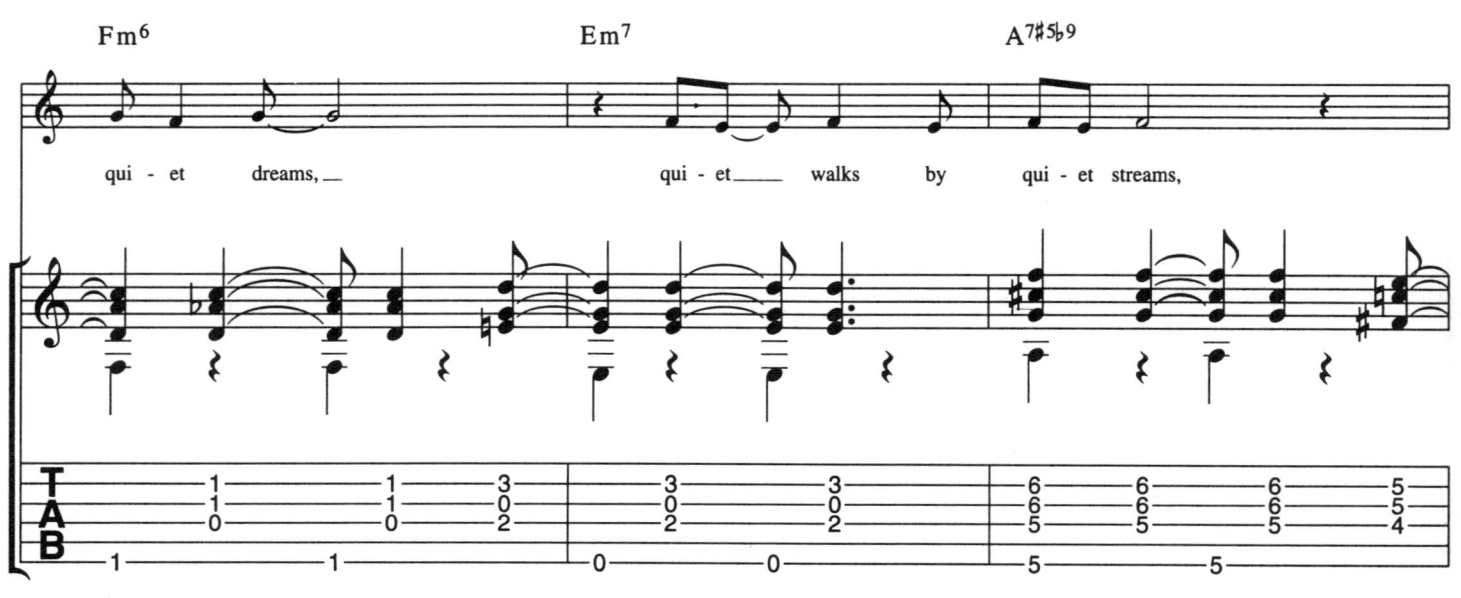

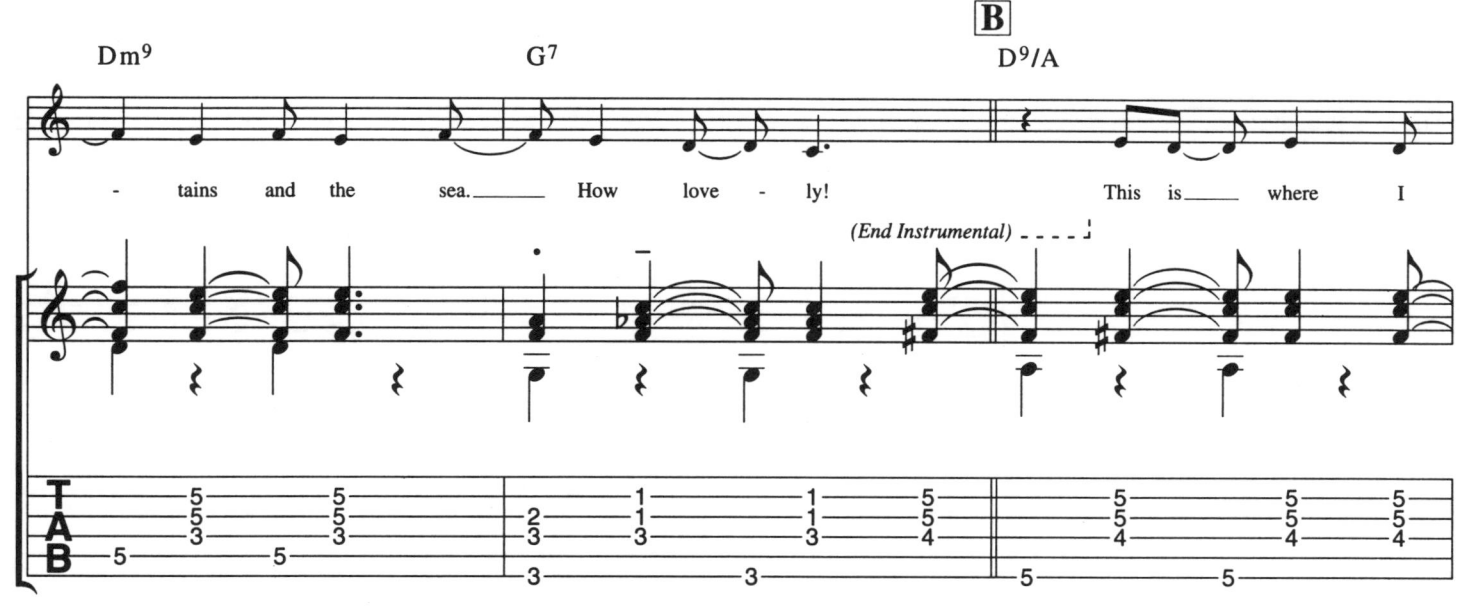
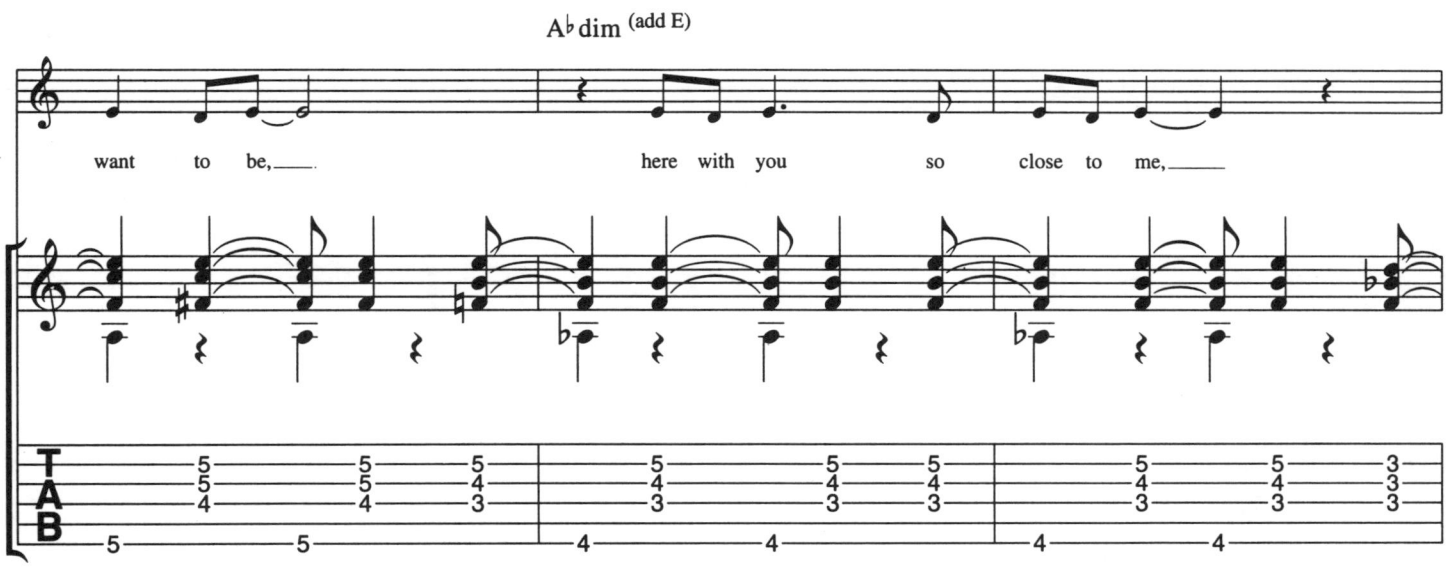
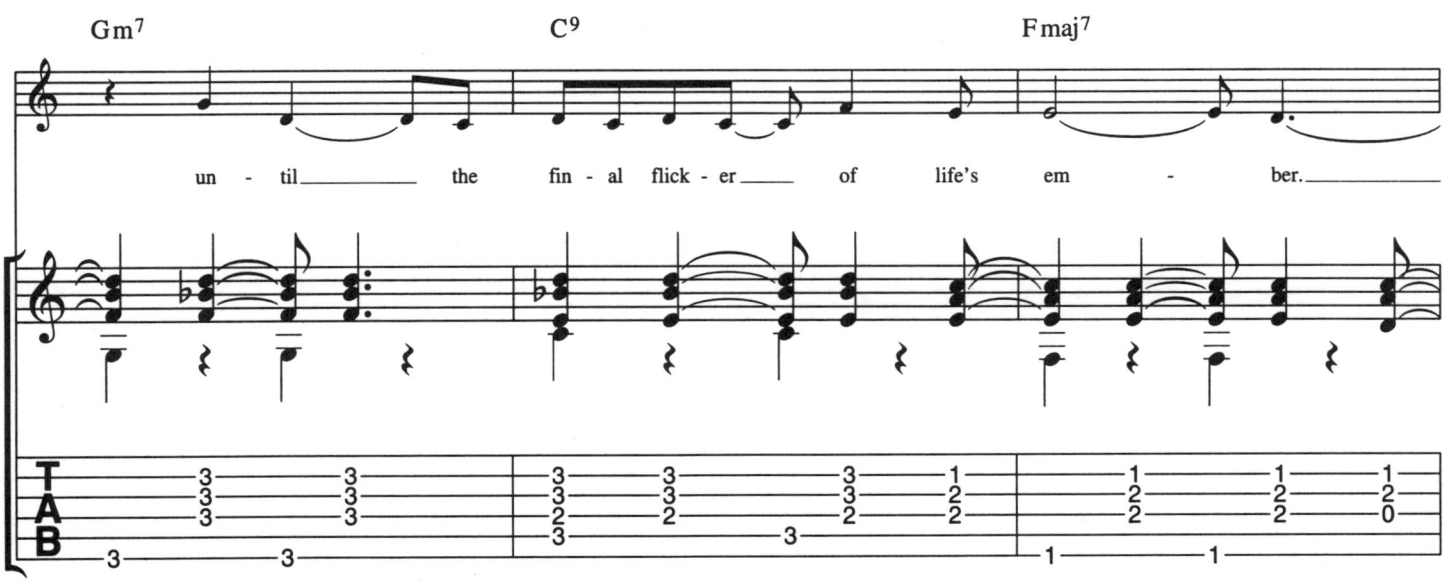

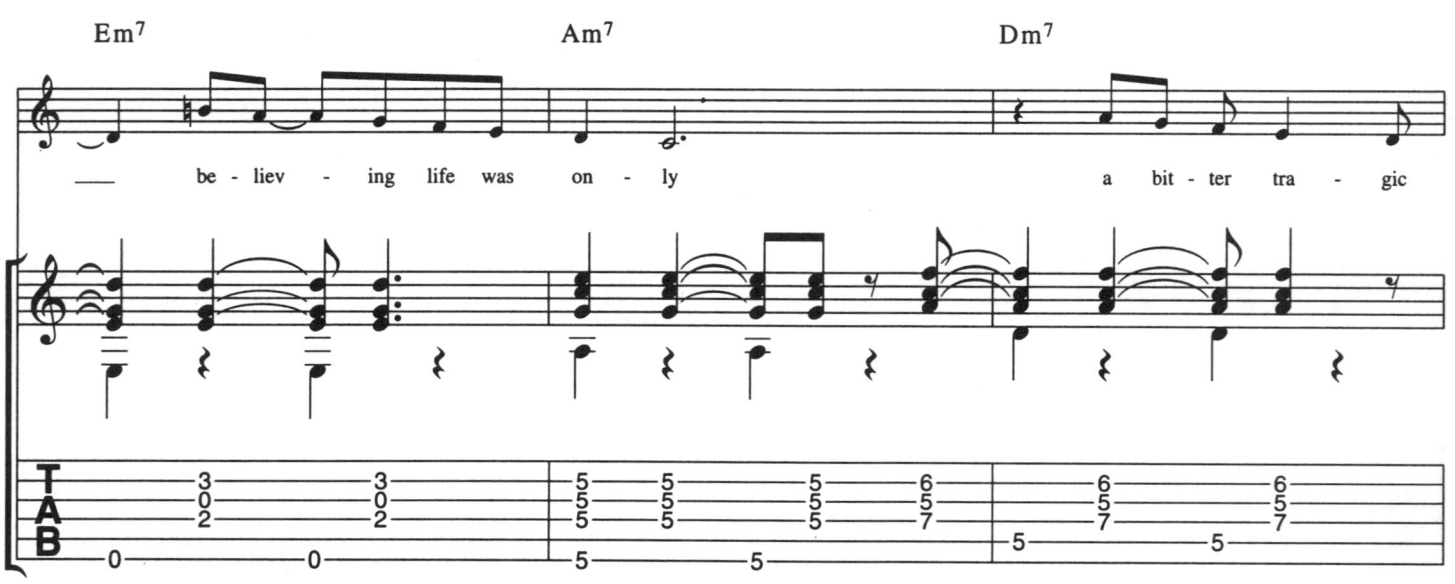

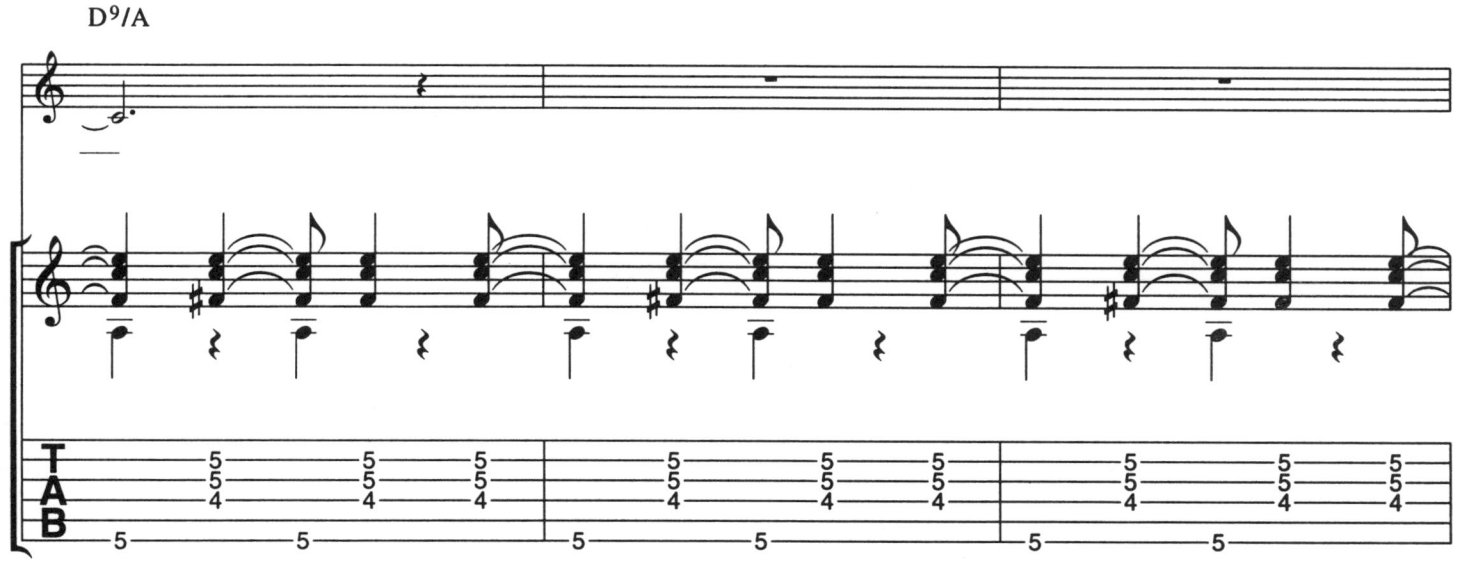
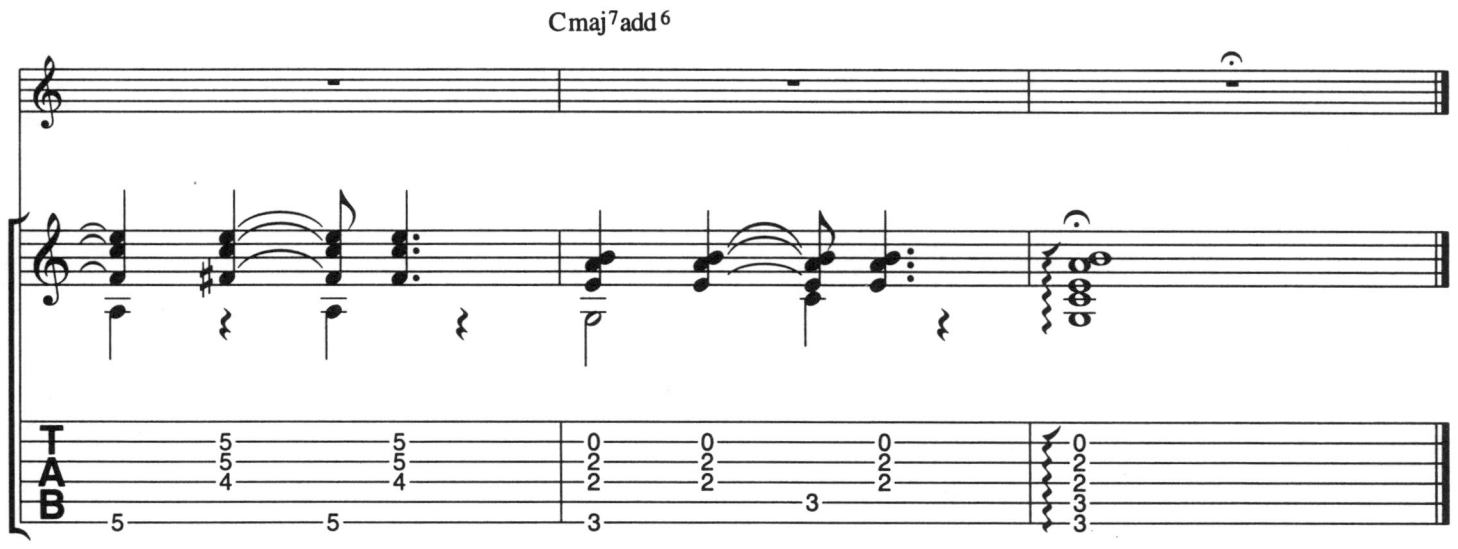

how insensitive
(insensatez)

music by antonio carlos jobim
original lyrics by vinicius de moraes
english lyrics by norman gimbel

Allow the melody in this piece to sit gently with the chord accompaniment, which should be languid and allowed to flow.

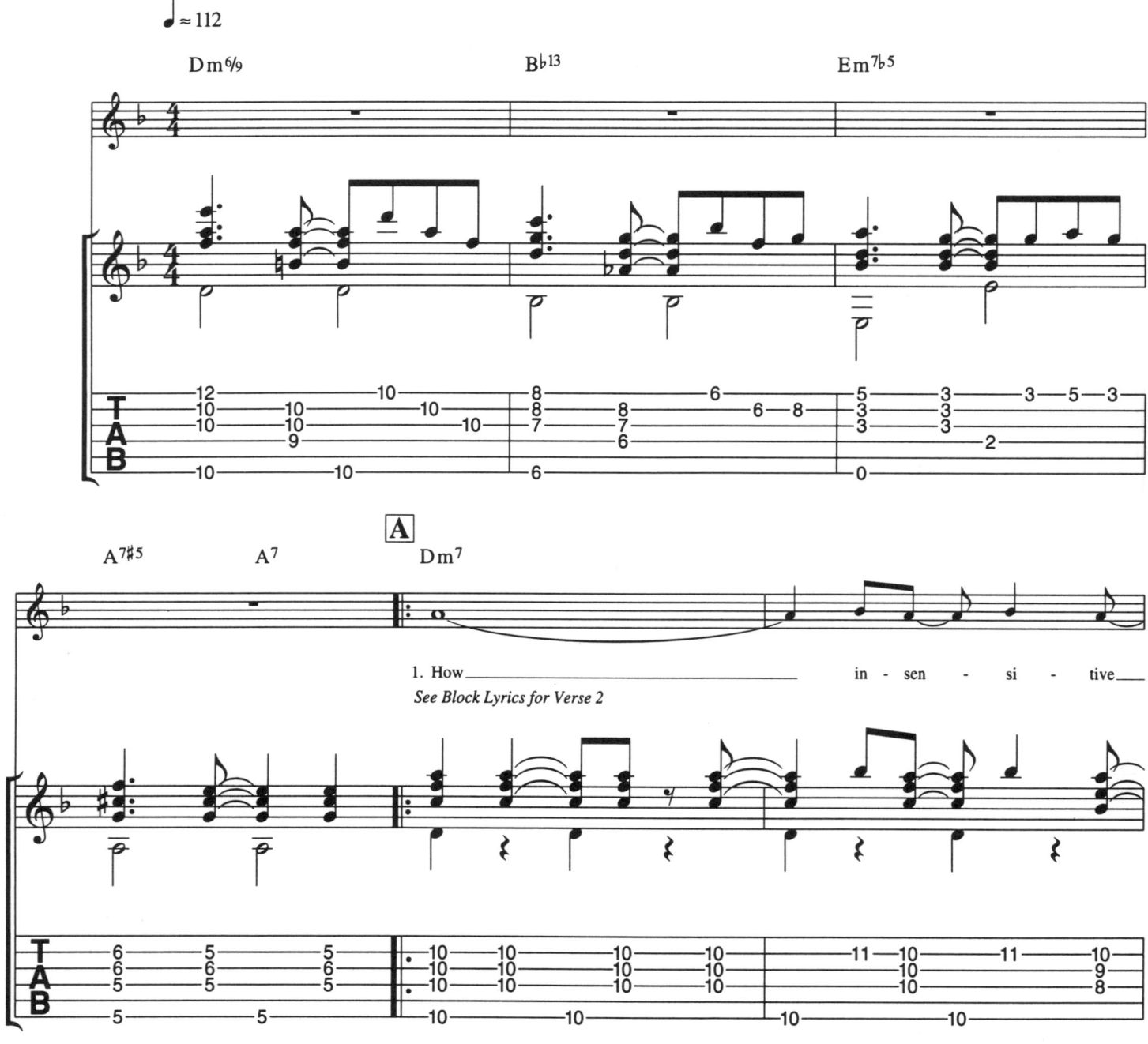

© copyright 1963, 1964 by antonio carlos jobim and vinicius de moraes, brazil
mca music limited, 77 fulham palace road, london w6 for the british commonwealth
(excluding canada), south africa, continent of europe (excluding italy, france, its colonies, protectorates
and mandated territories, algeria, tunisia, morocco, andorra and monaco)
all rights reserved
international copyright secured

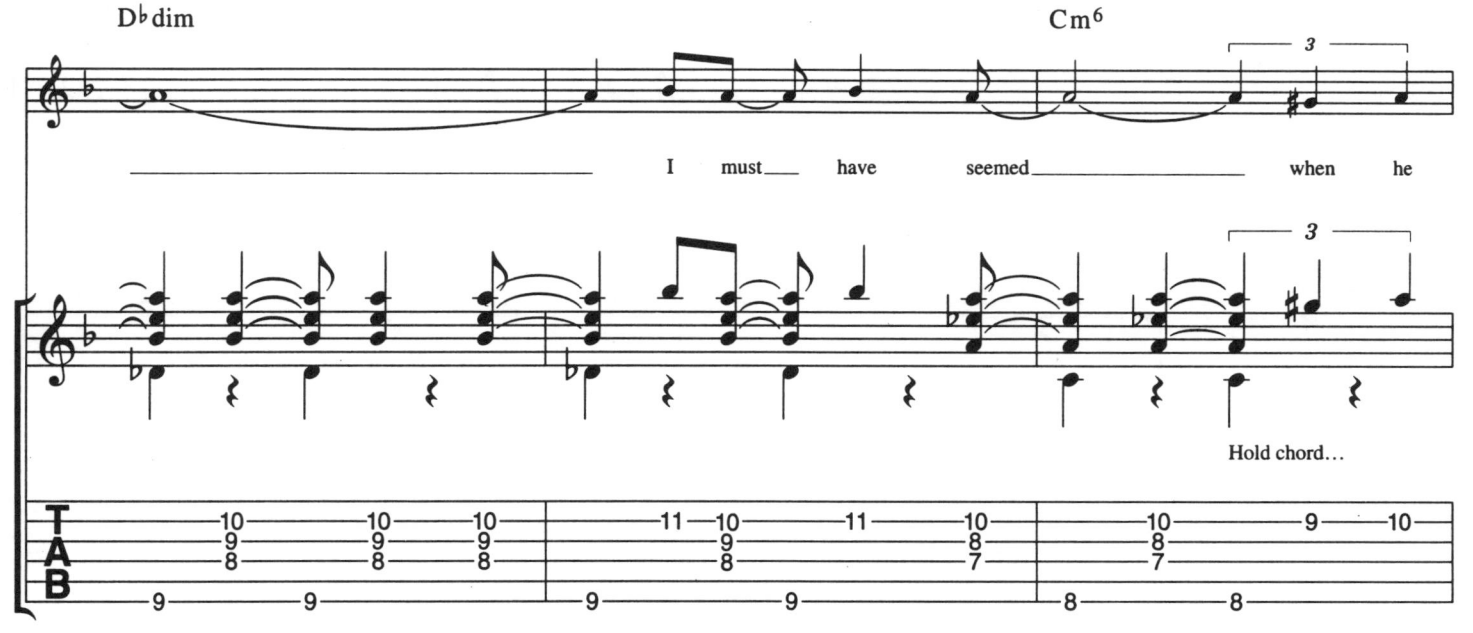

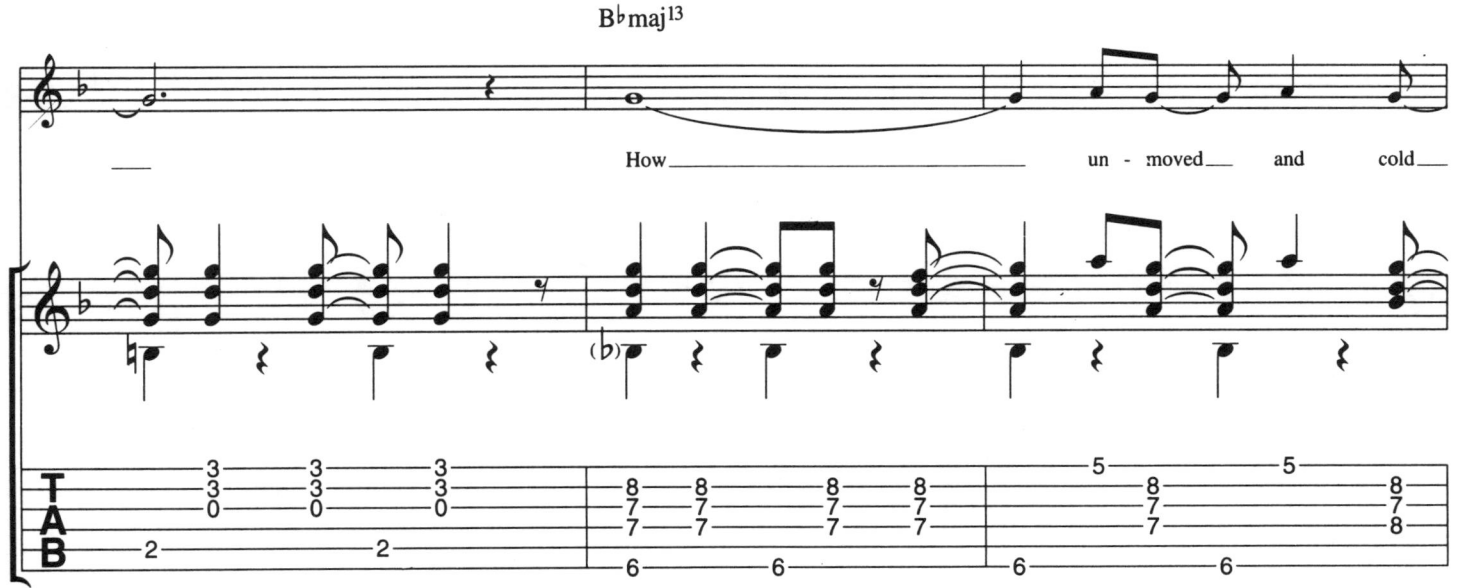

13

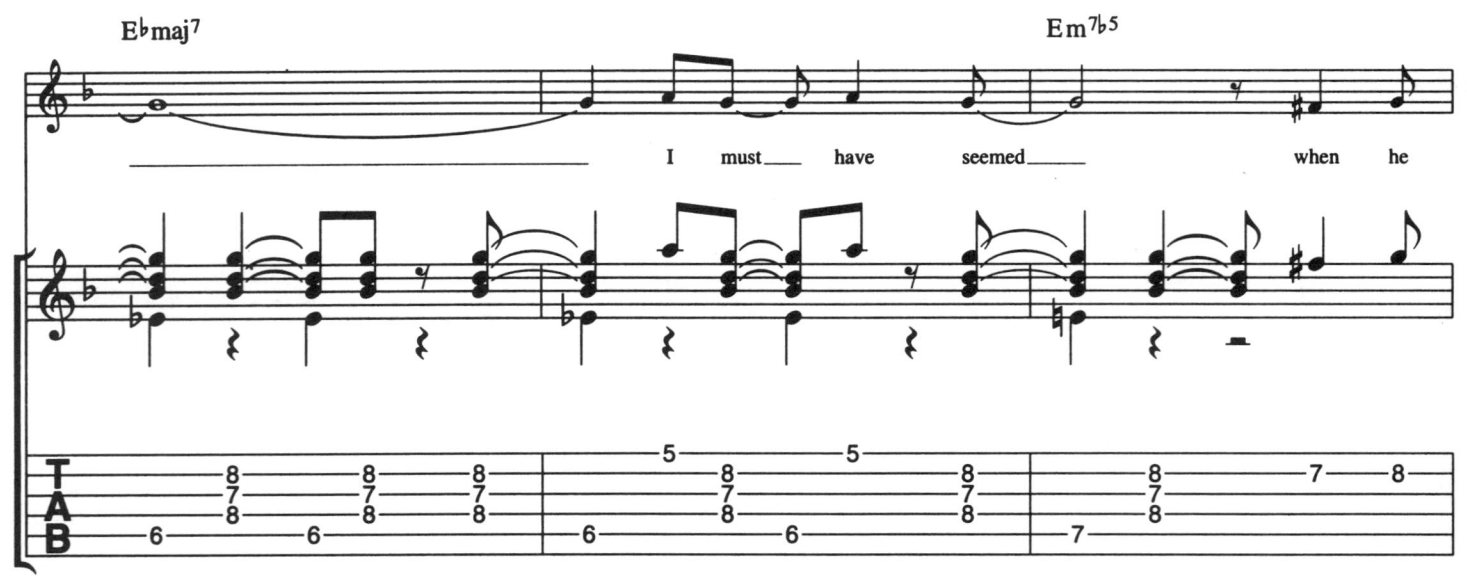
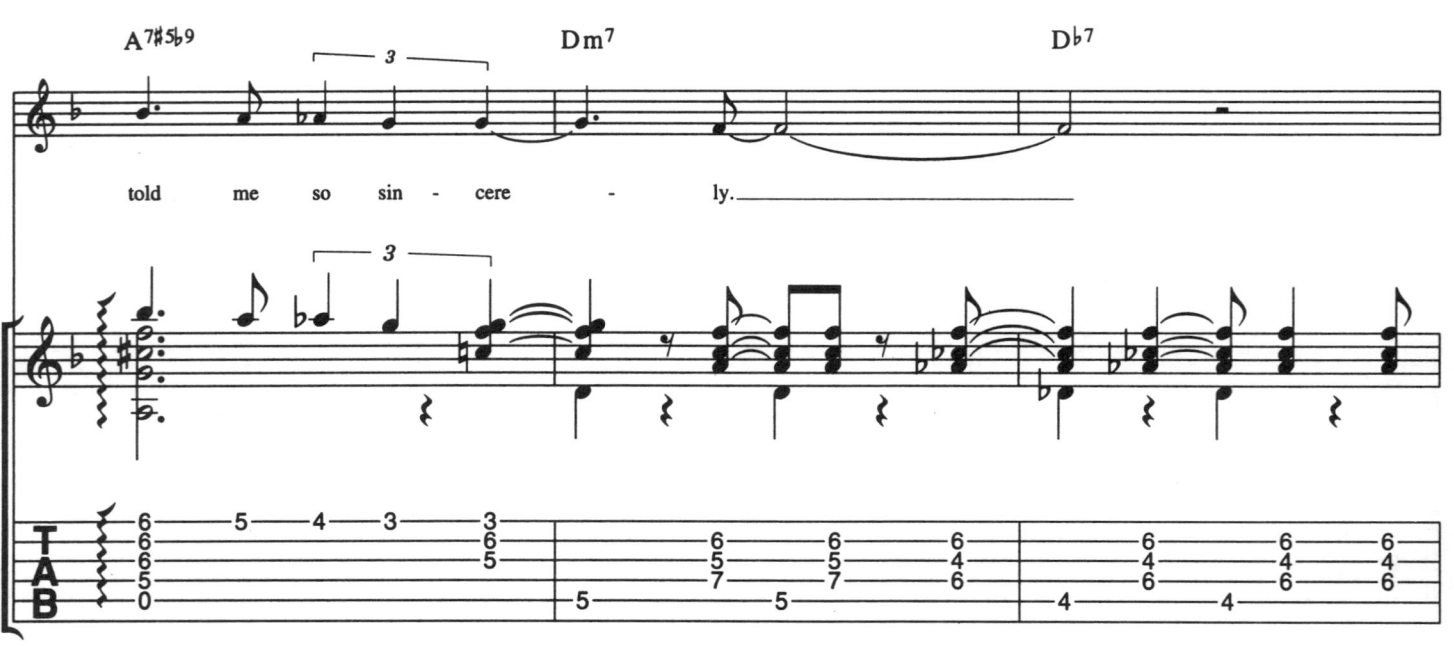

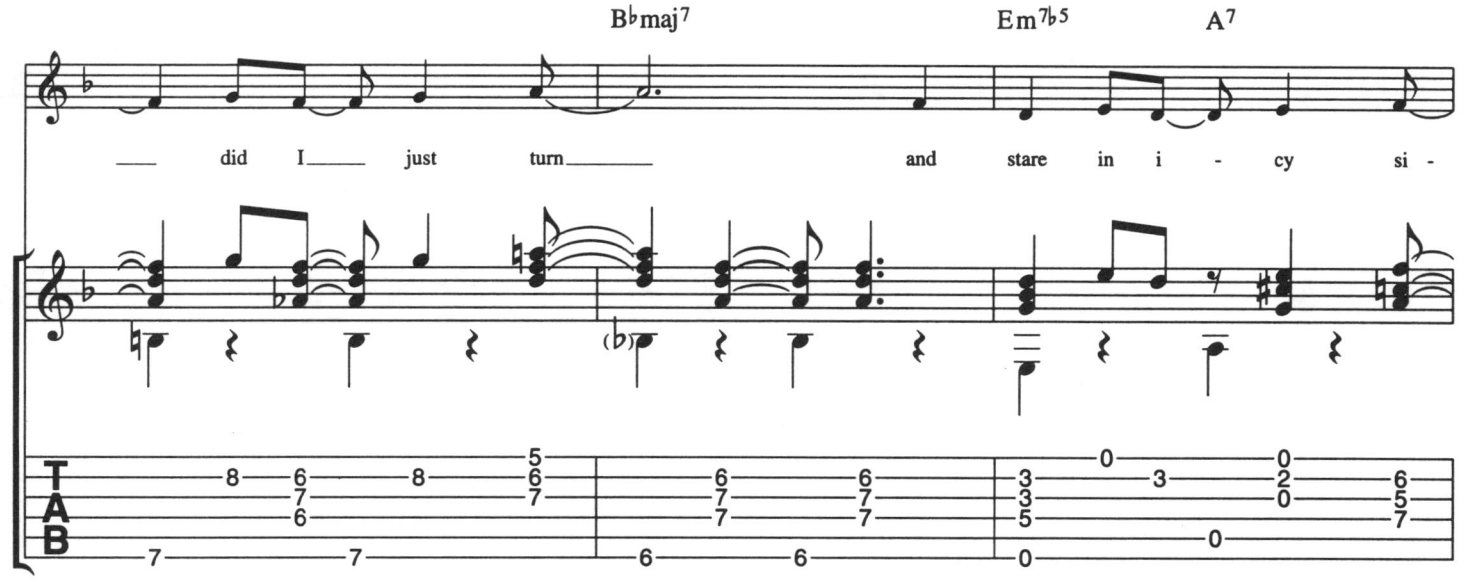
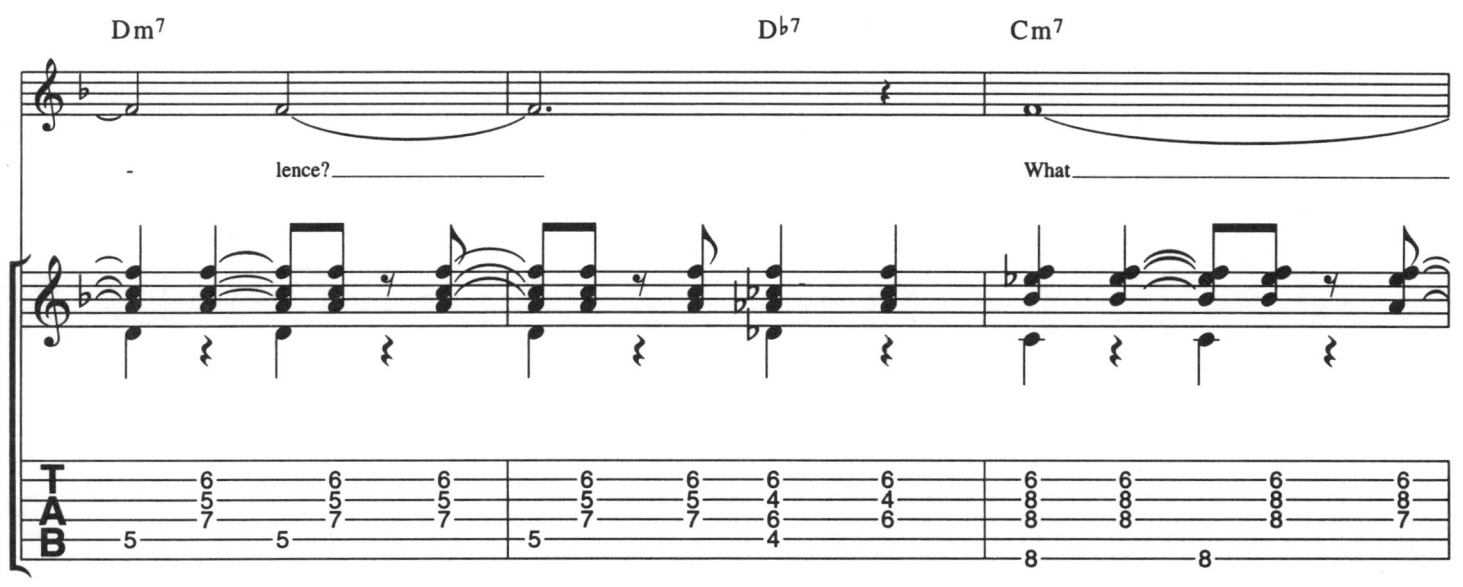
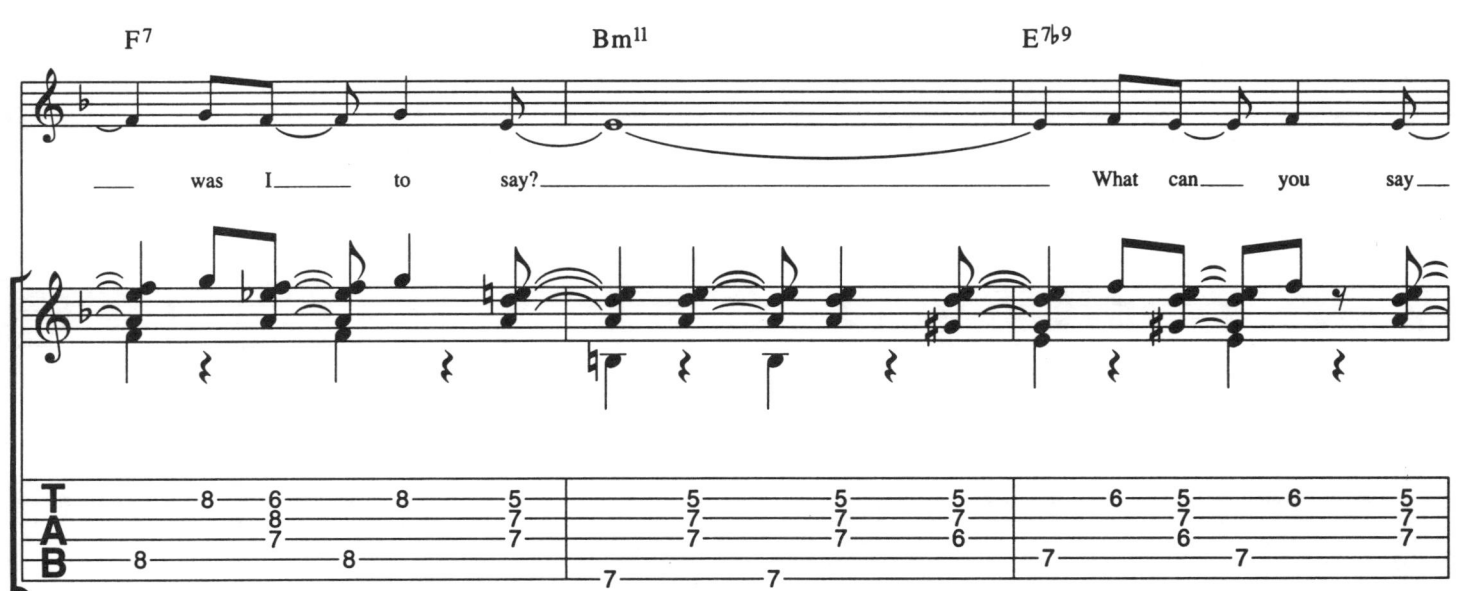

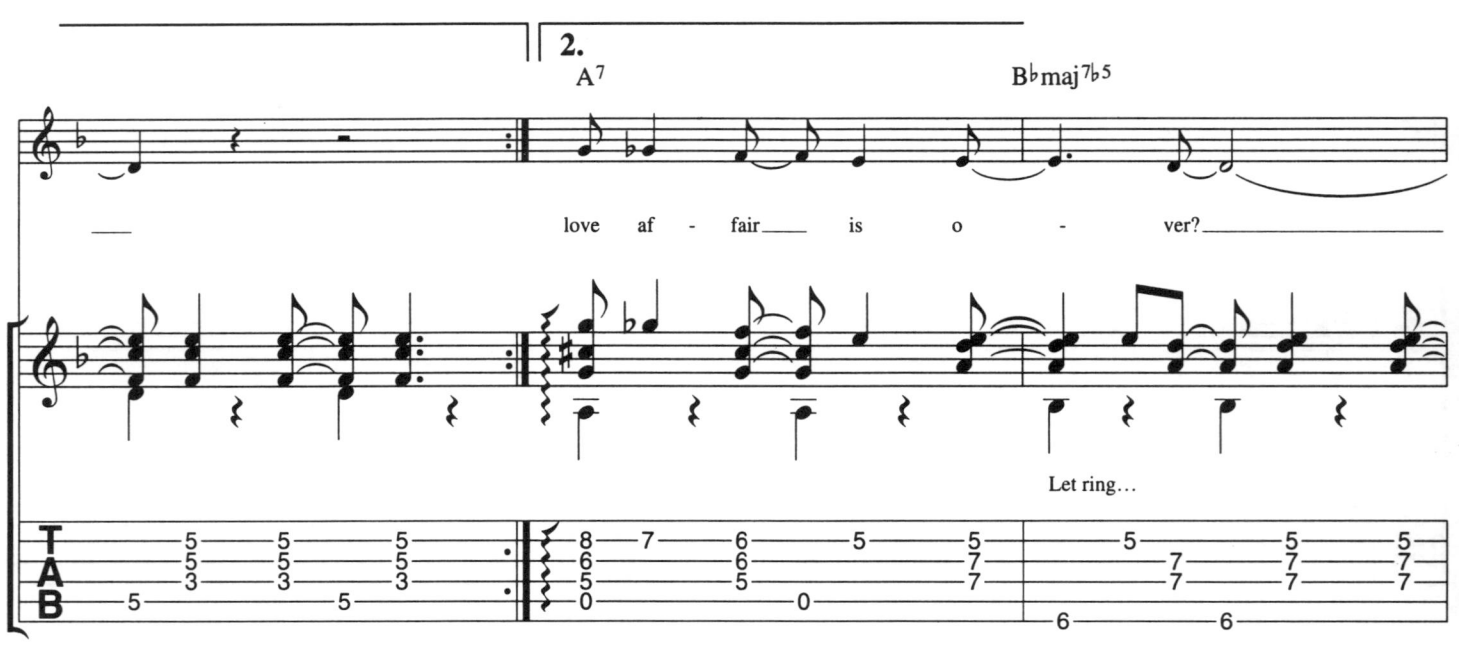
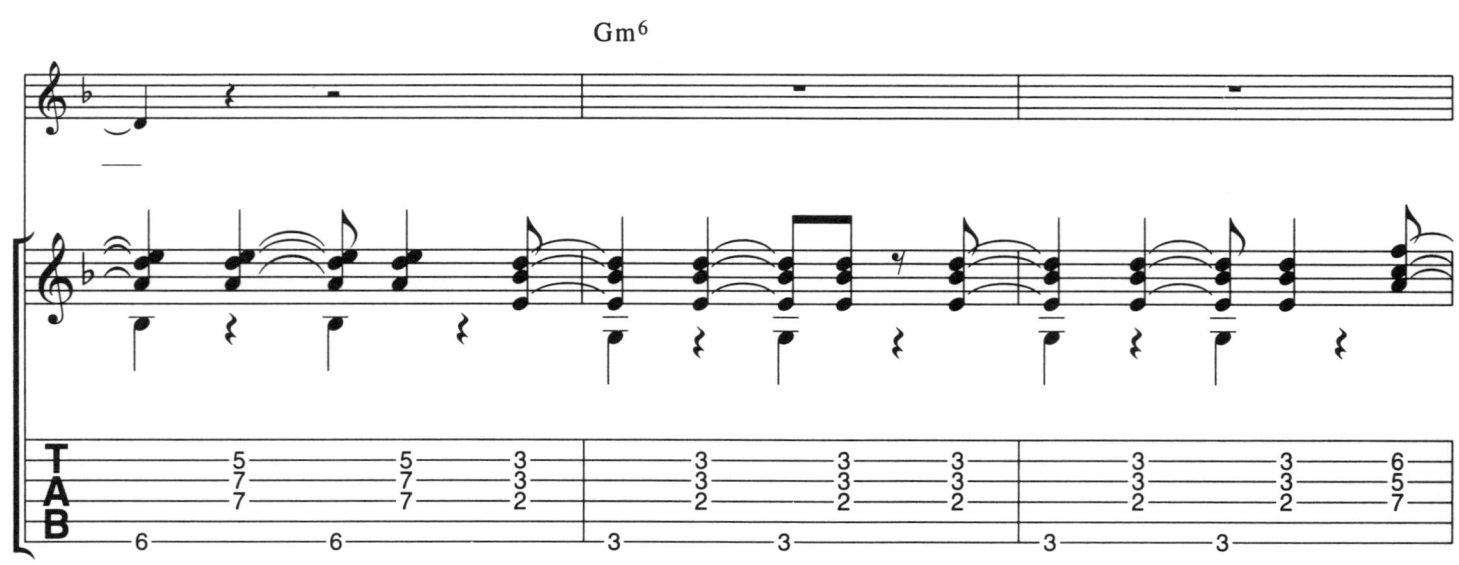

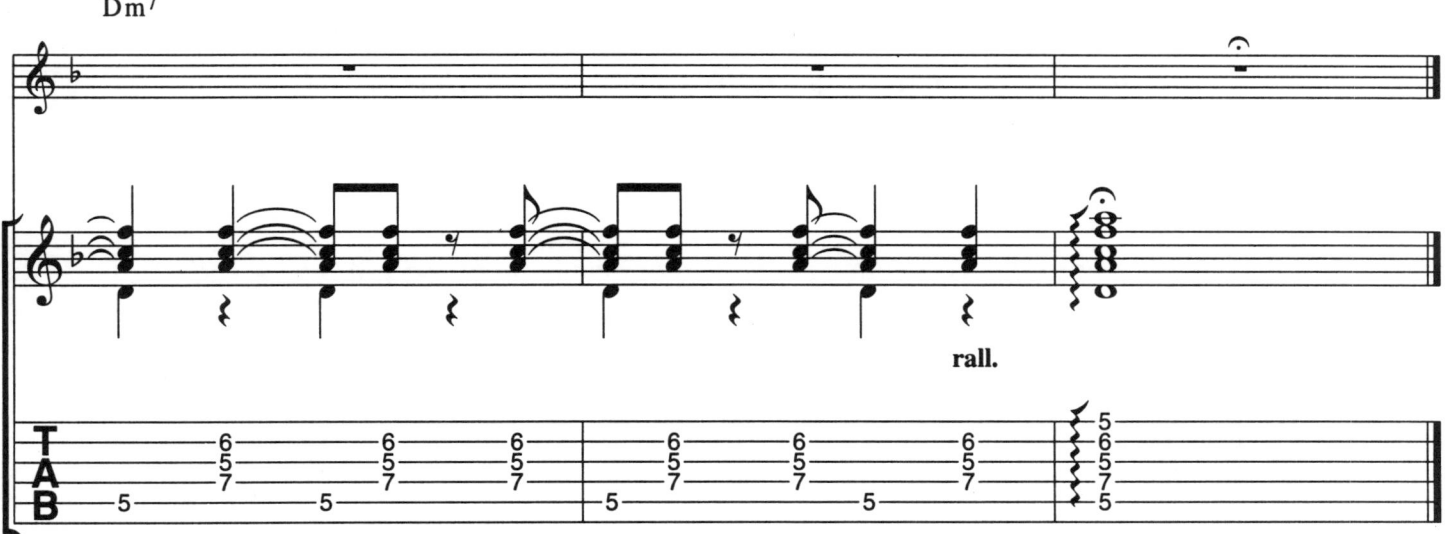

Verse 2:
Now, he's gone away
And I'm alone
With the mem'ry of his last look
Vague and drawn and sad
I see it still
All his heartbreak in that last look
How, he must have asked
Could I just turn
And stare in icy silence?
What was I to do?
What can one do
When a love affair is over?

Portuguese lyrics

A insensatez
Que você fez
Coração mais sem cuidado
Fez chorar de dõr
O seu amõr
Um amõr tão delicado
Ah! Porque você
Foi fraco assim
Assim tão desalmado
Ah! Meu coração
Que nunca amou
Não merece ser amado
Vai meu coração
Ouve a razão
Usa só sinceridade
Quem semeia vento
Diz a razão
Colhe tempestade
Vai meu coração
Pede perdão
Perdão apaixonado
Vai porque
Quem não
Pede perdão
Não é nunca perdoado.

if you never come to me
(inutil paisagem)

music & original words by antonio carlos jobim
english lyric by ray gilbert

The chord progression in this piece was originally recorded with voice and piano. To achieve the feel, relax and lay back on the tempo.

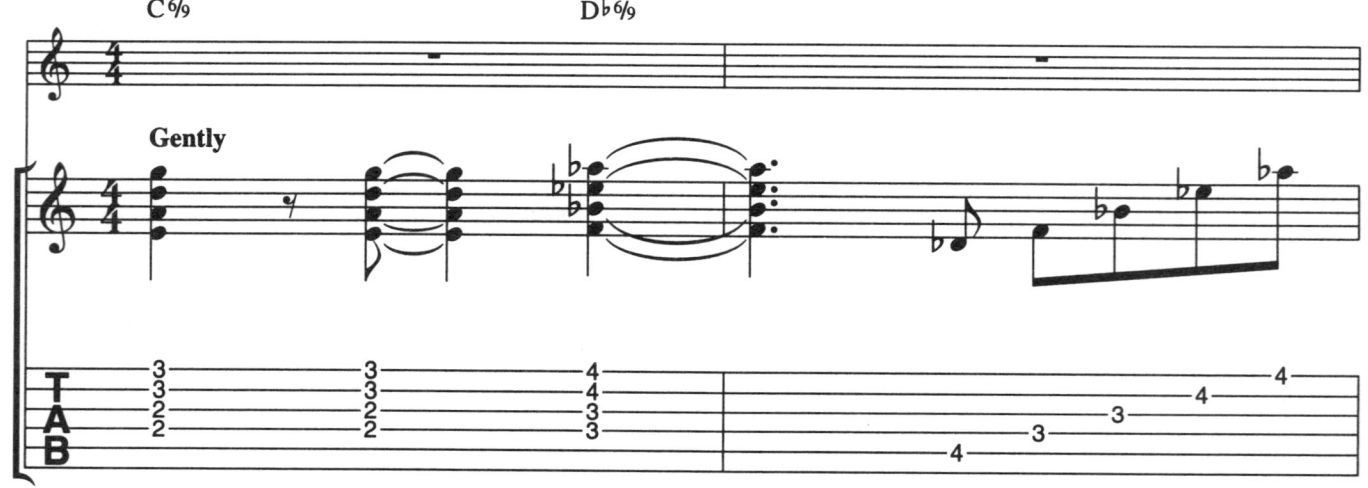

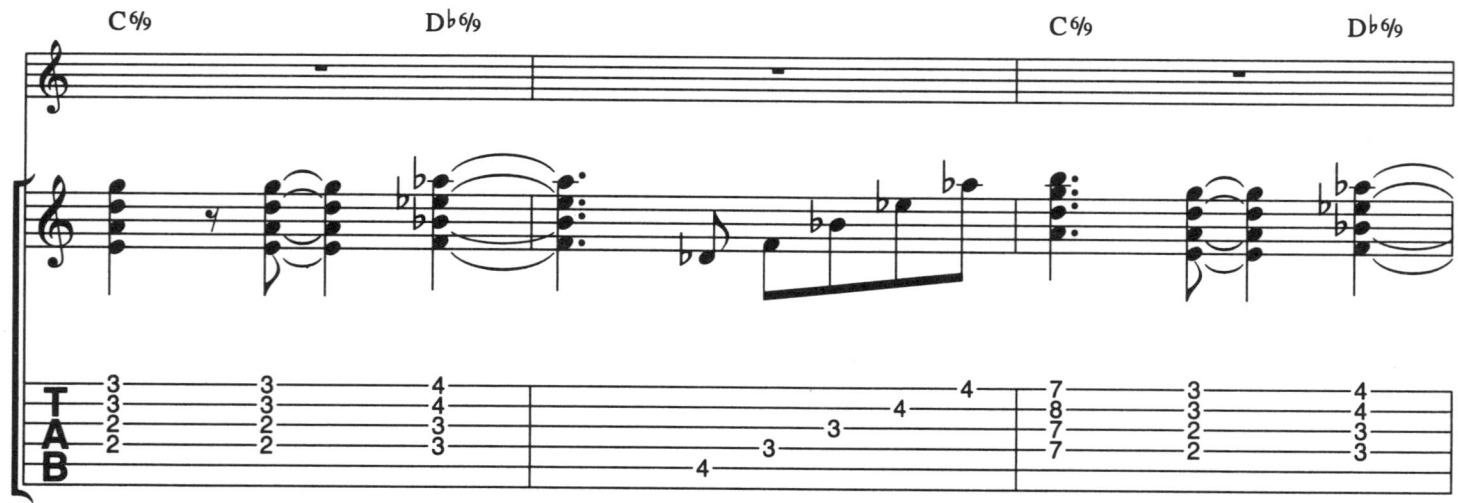

© copyright 1965 ipanema music company, usa
sparta florida music group limited, 8/9 frith street, london w1
all rights reserved
international copyright secured

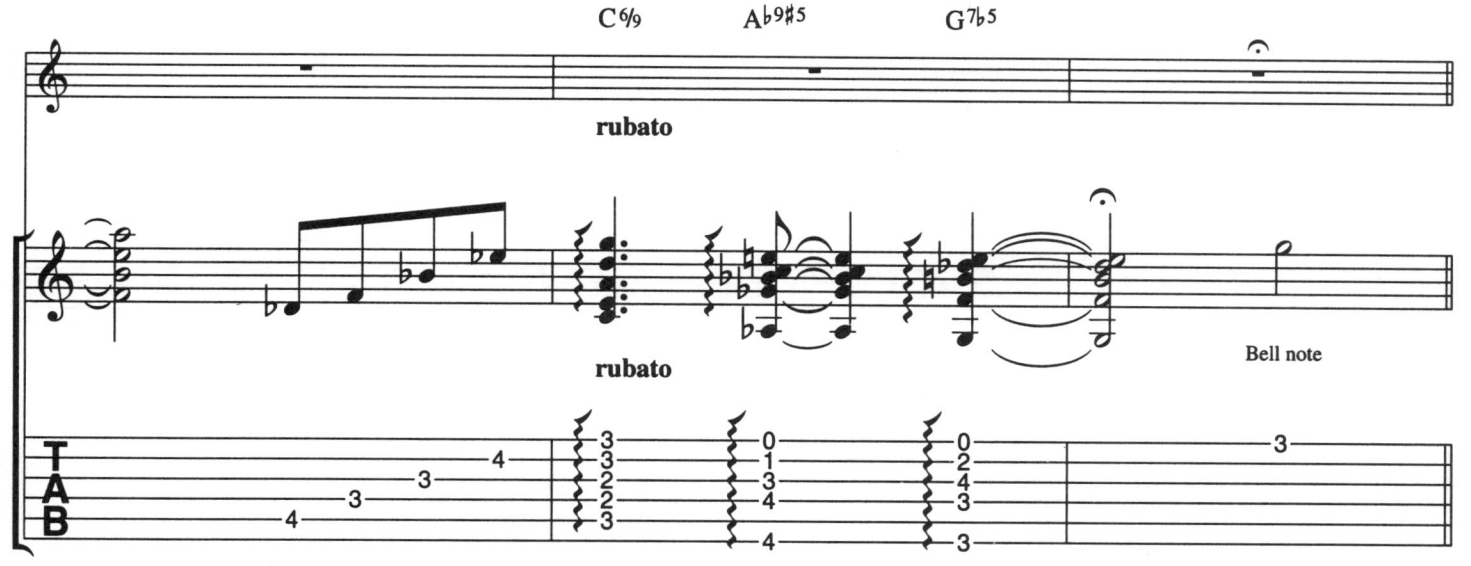

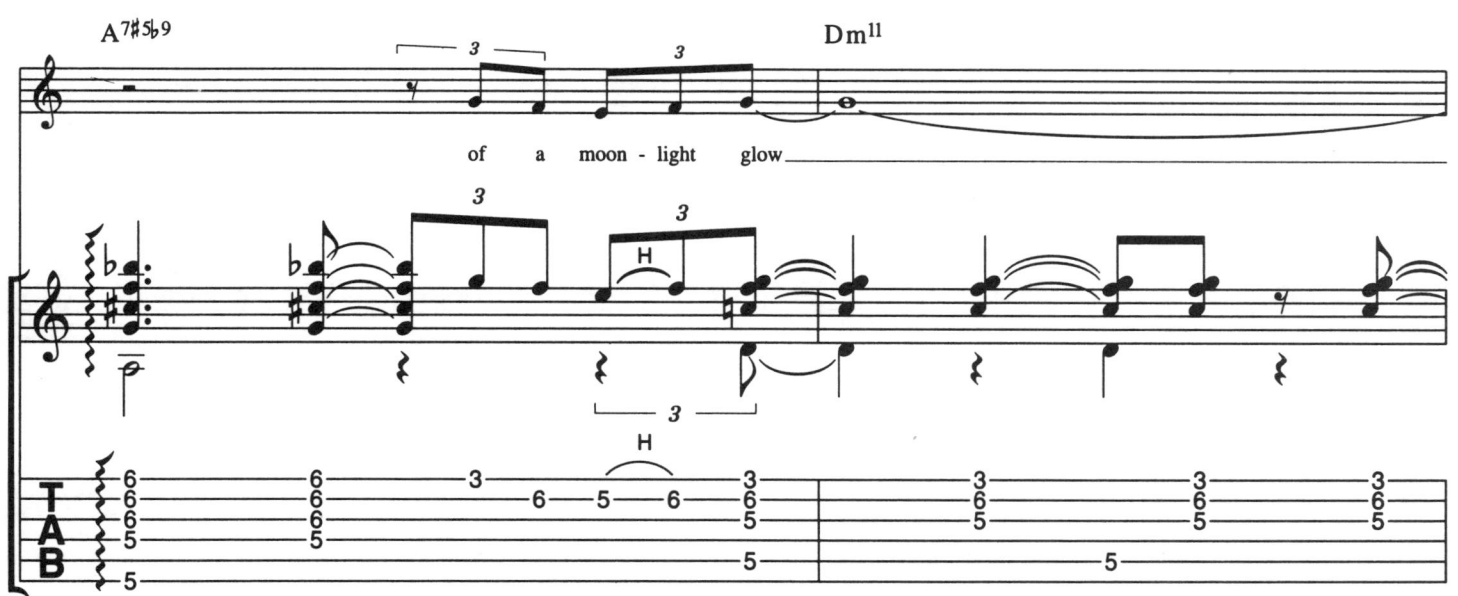

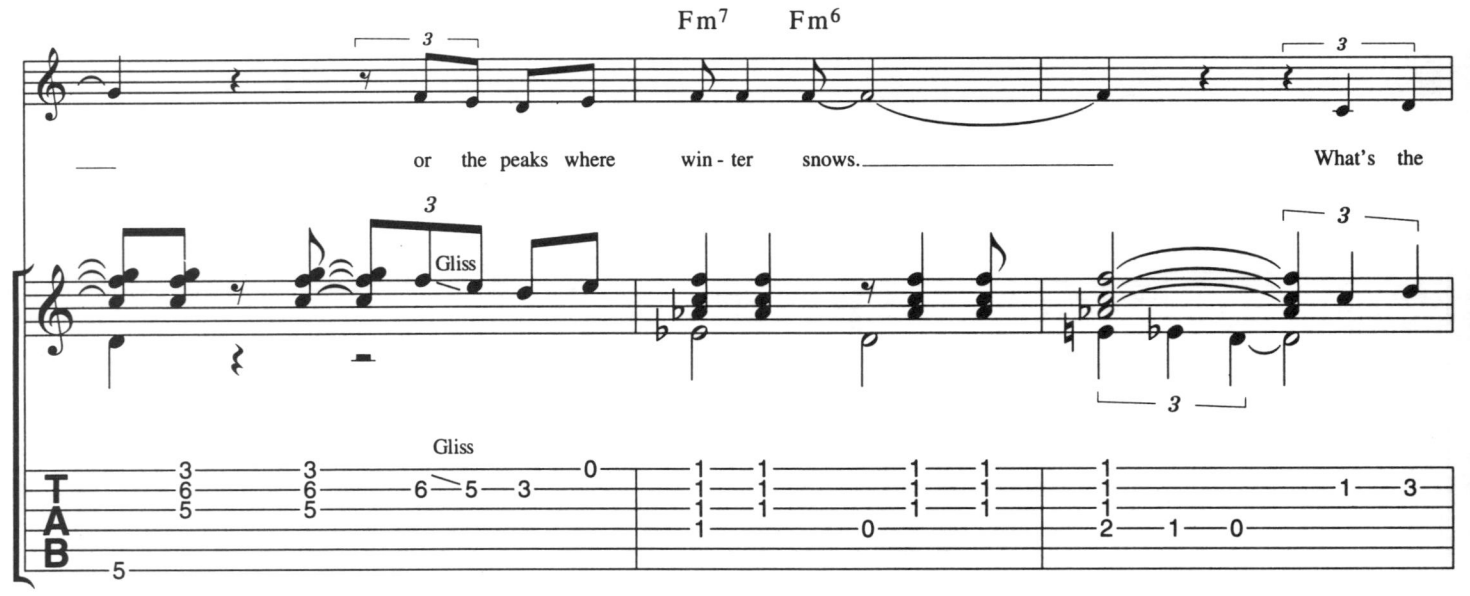

F7#9
Cmaj7
Db9#11
out you? It's no - thing.
B
Cmaj7
Bmaj7#13
Bbmajb5
1. It may be
2.(𝄋) Ad lib. Instrumental
A7#5b9
Dm11
you will ne - ver come,
H
TAB

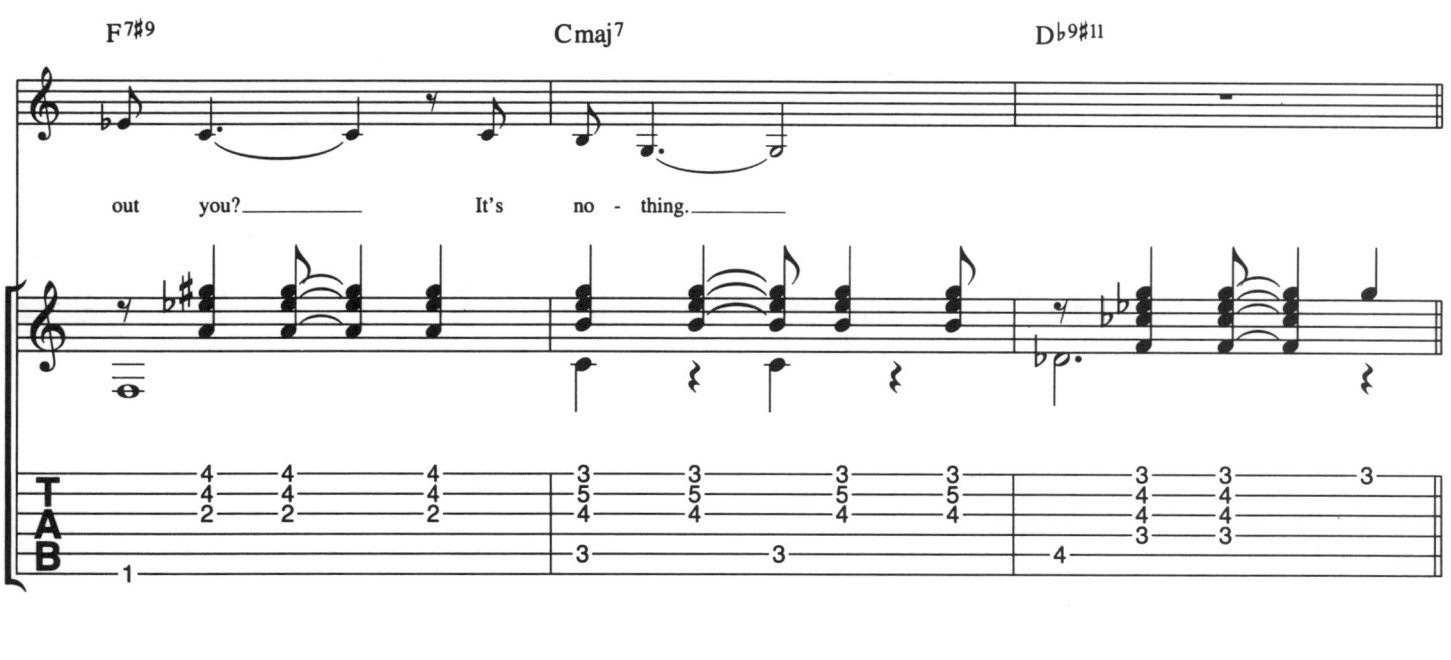

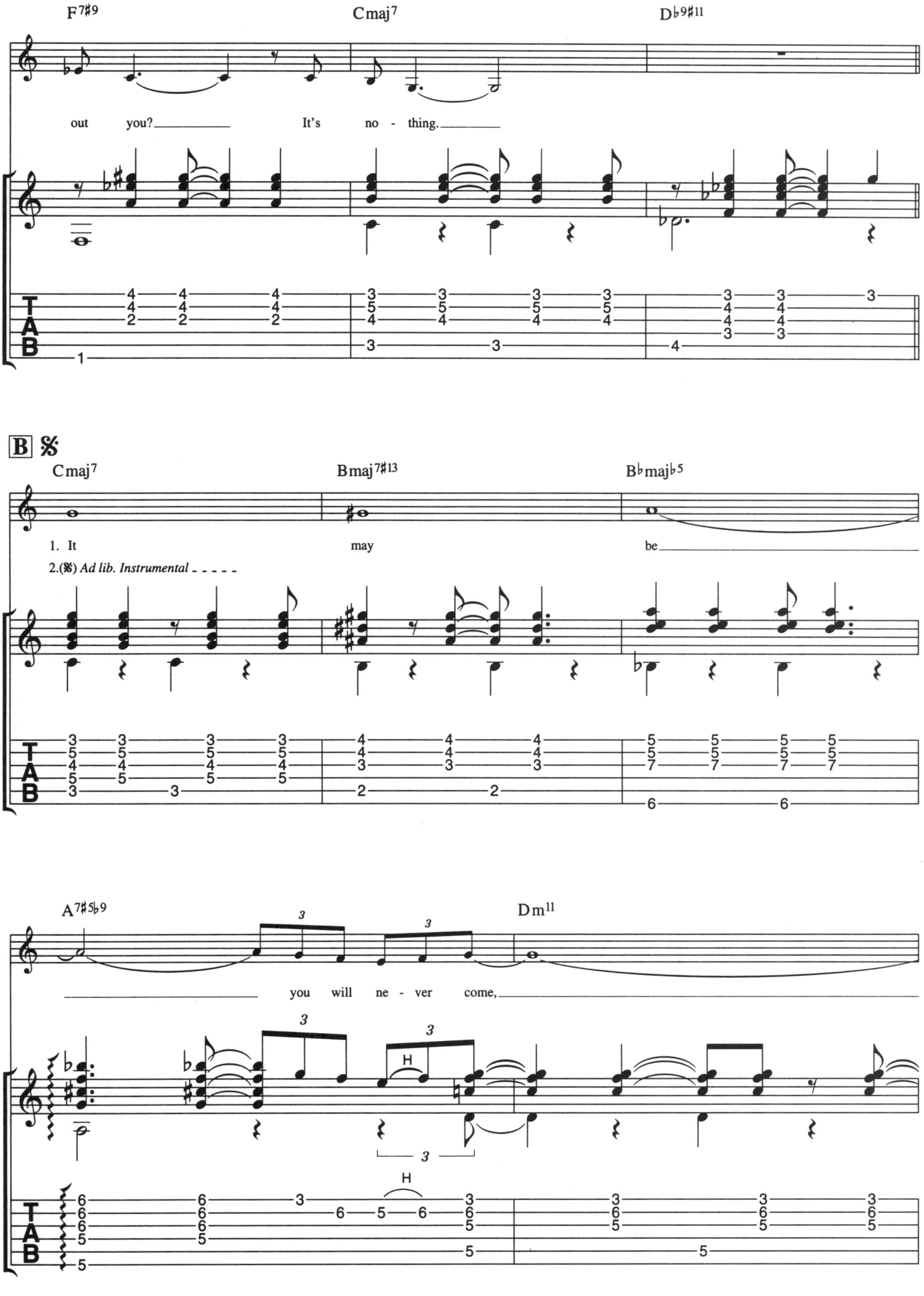

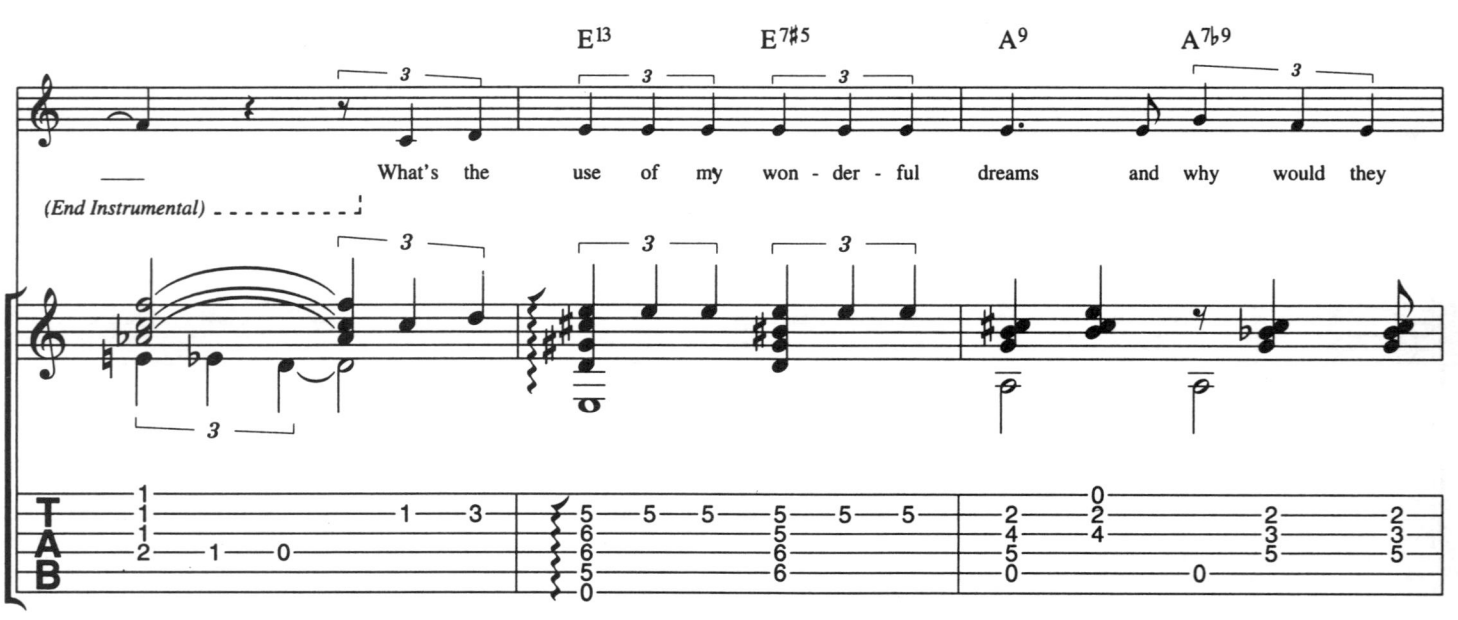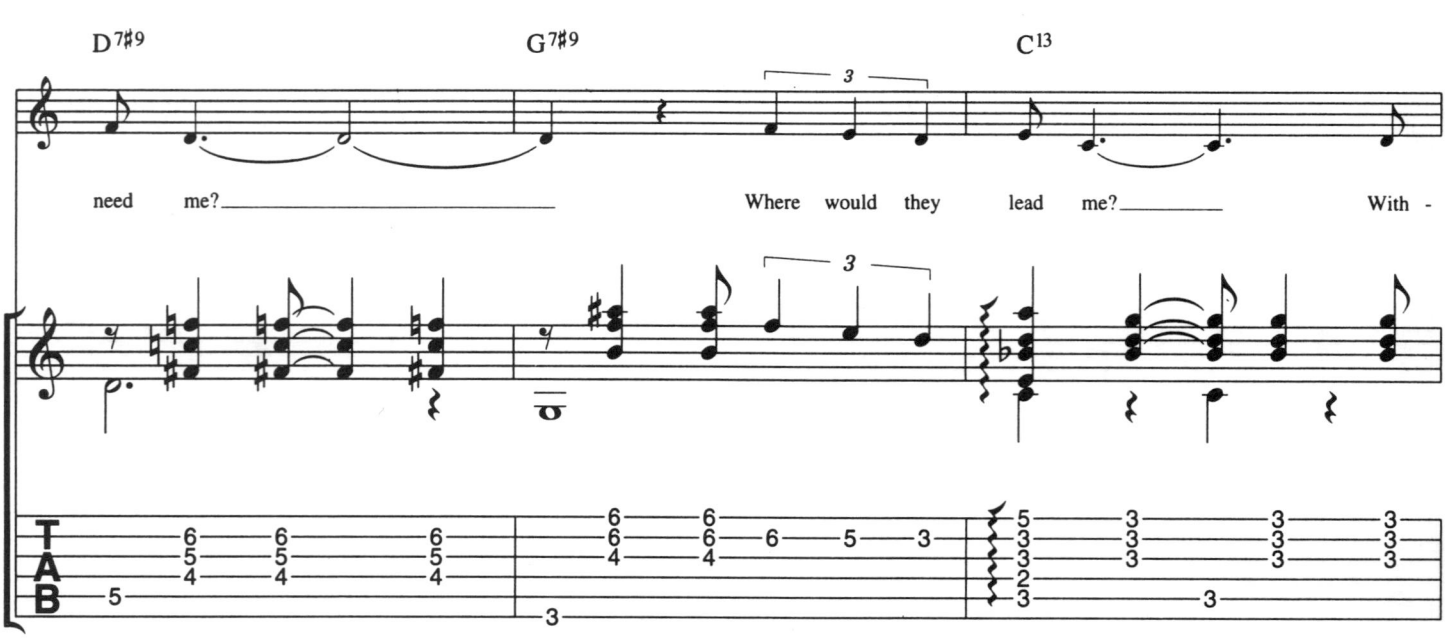

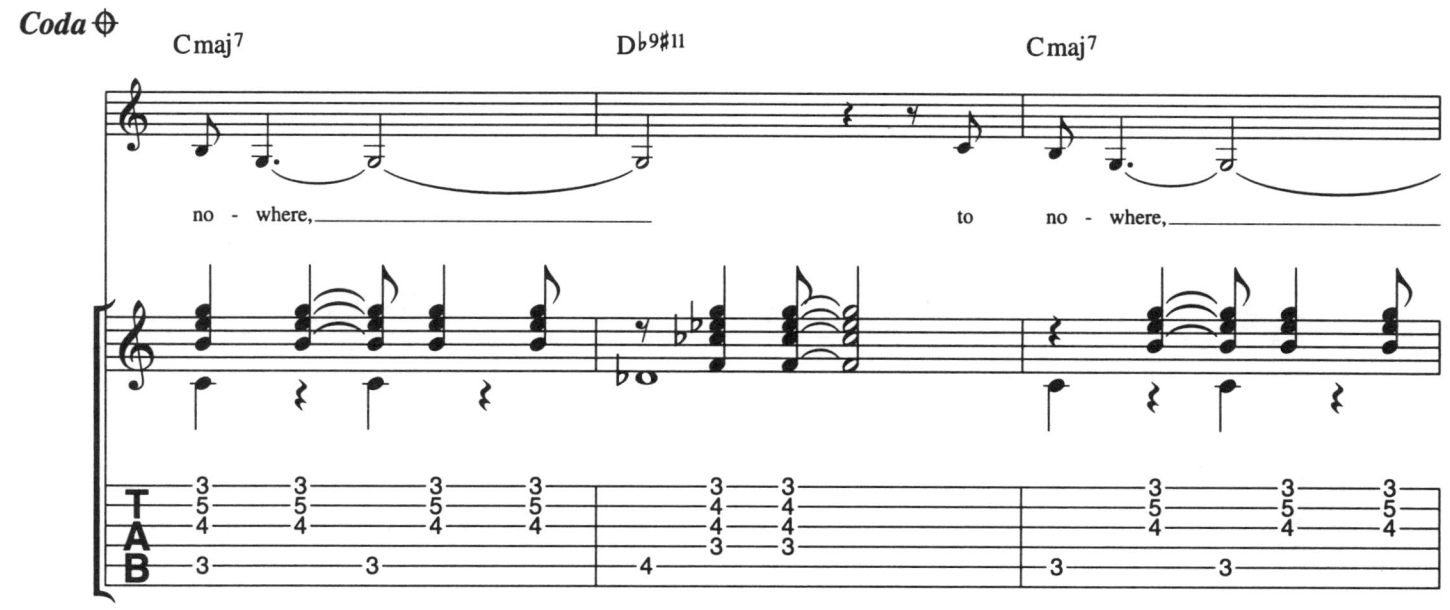

meditation
(meditaçao)

original words by newton mendonca
english lyric by norman gimbel
music by antonio carlos jobim

This piece should be played in a cool and contained style with the chord accompaniment gently supporting the melody. The original instrumental version was played on the piano.

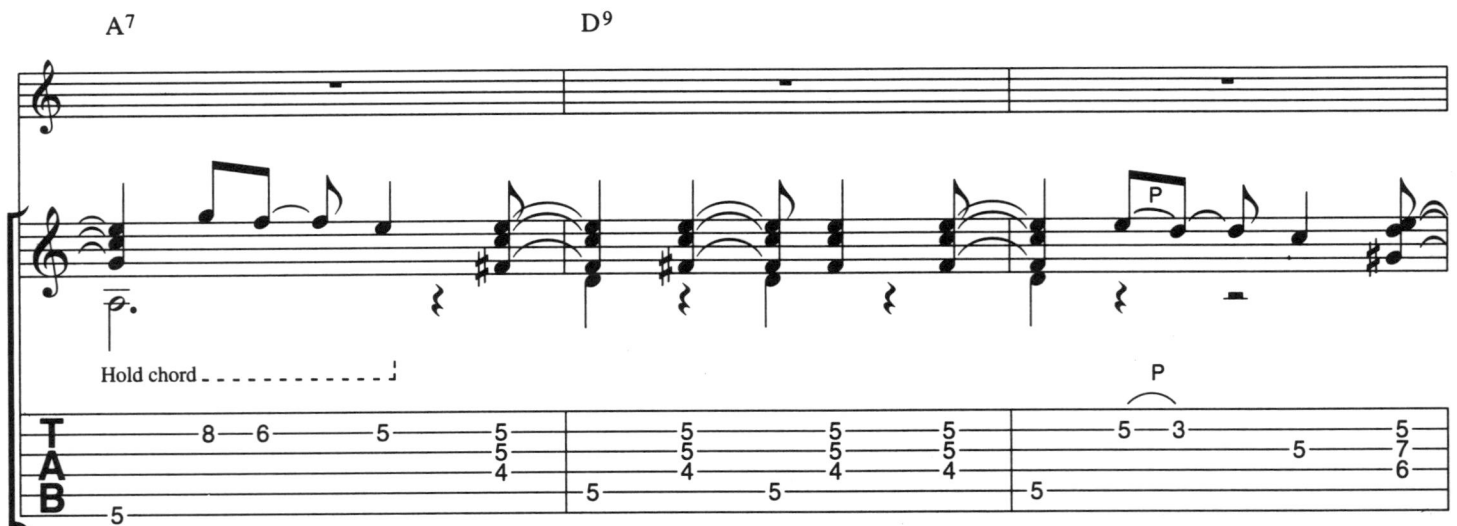

© copyright 1962,1963 antonio carlos jobim and mrs newton mendonca, brazil
mca music limited, 77 fulham palace road, london w6 for the british
commonwealth (excluding canada) south africa and eire
all rights reserved
international copyright secured

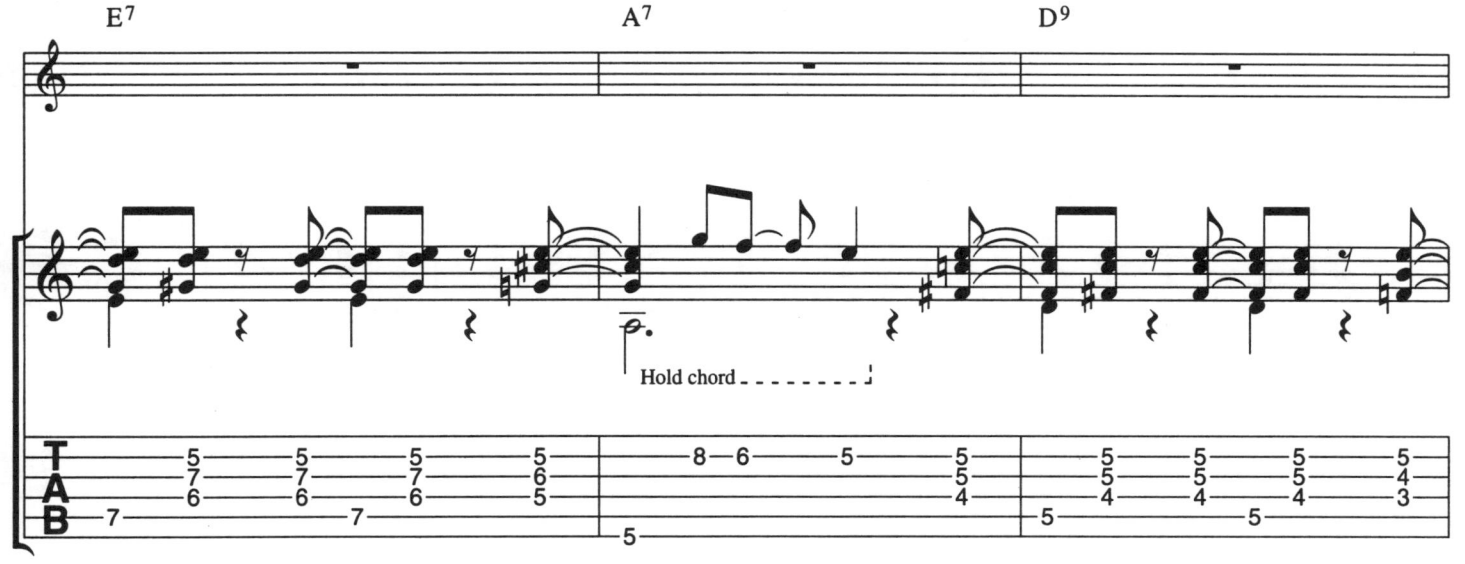
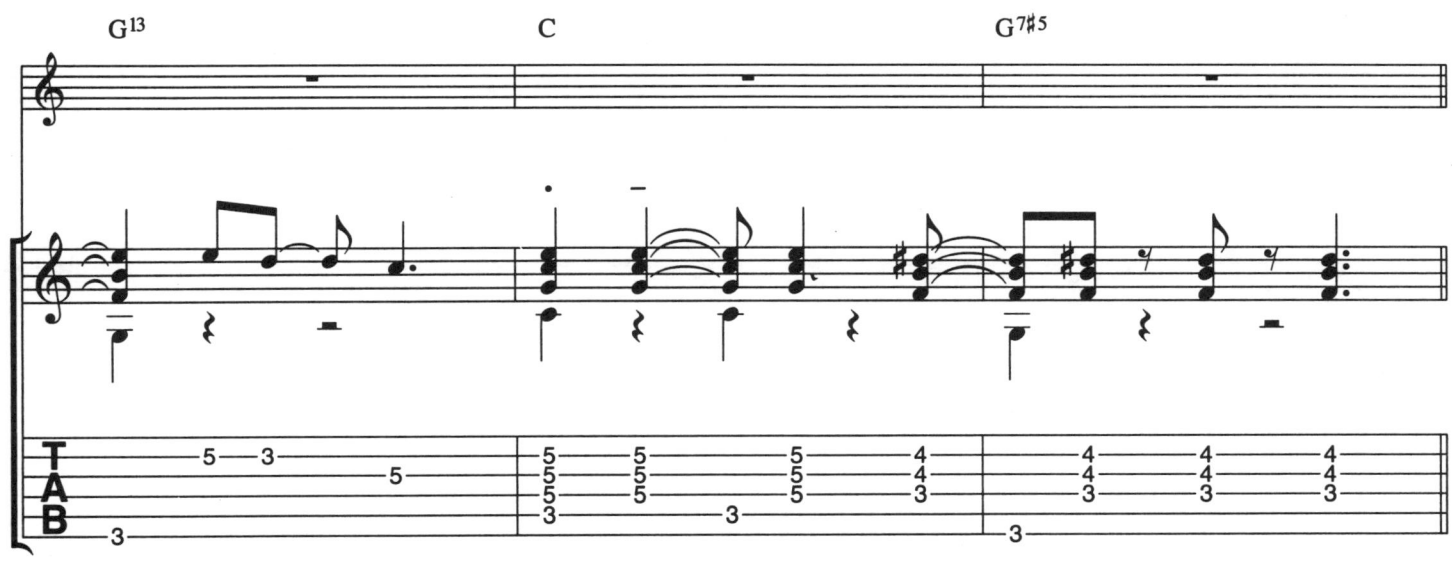

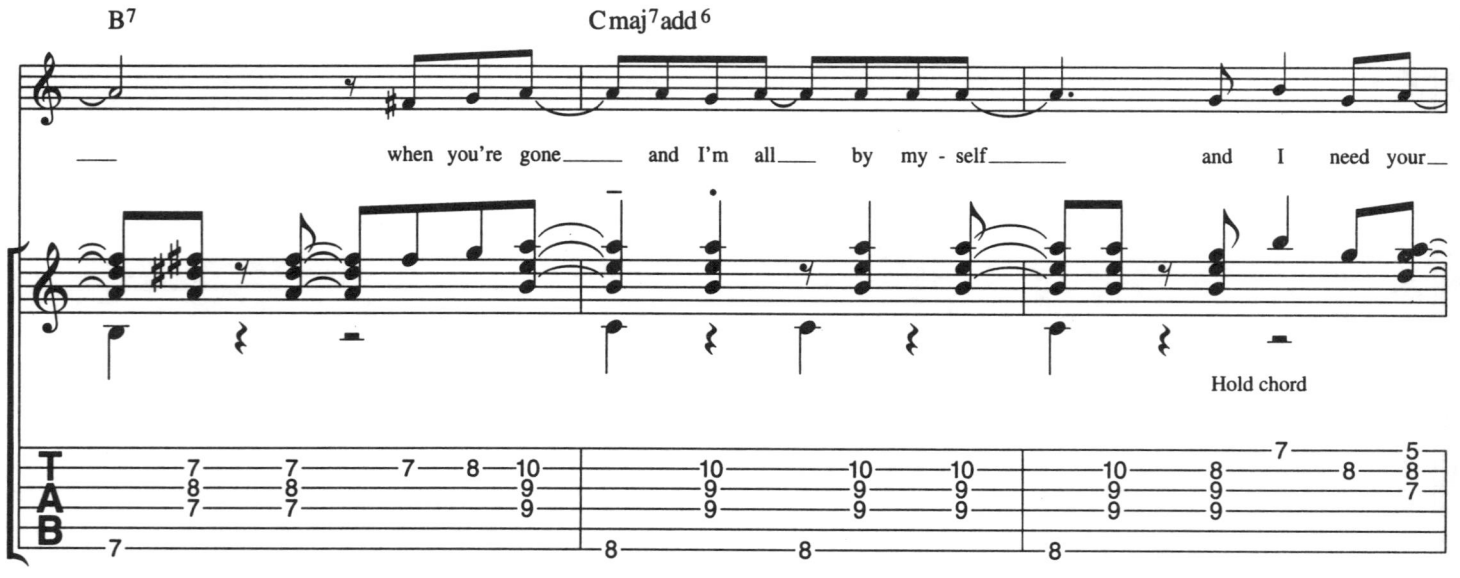
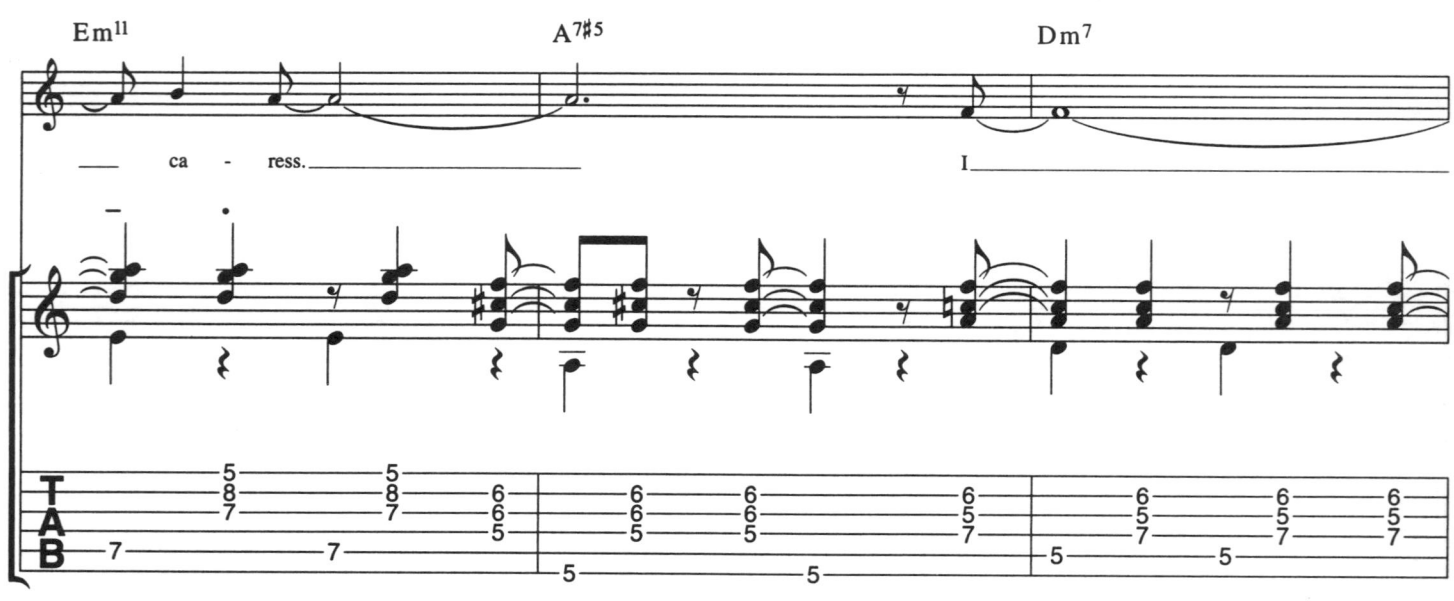

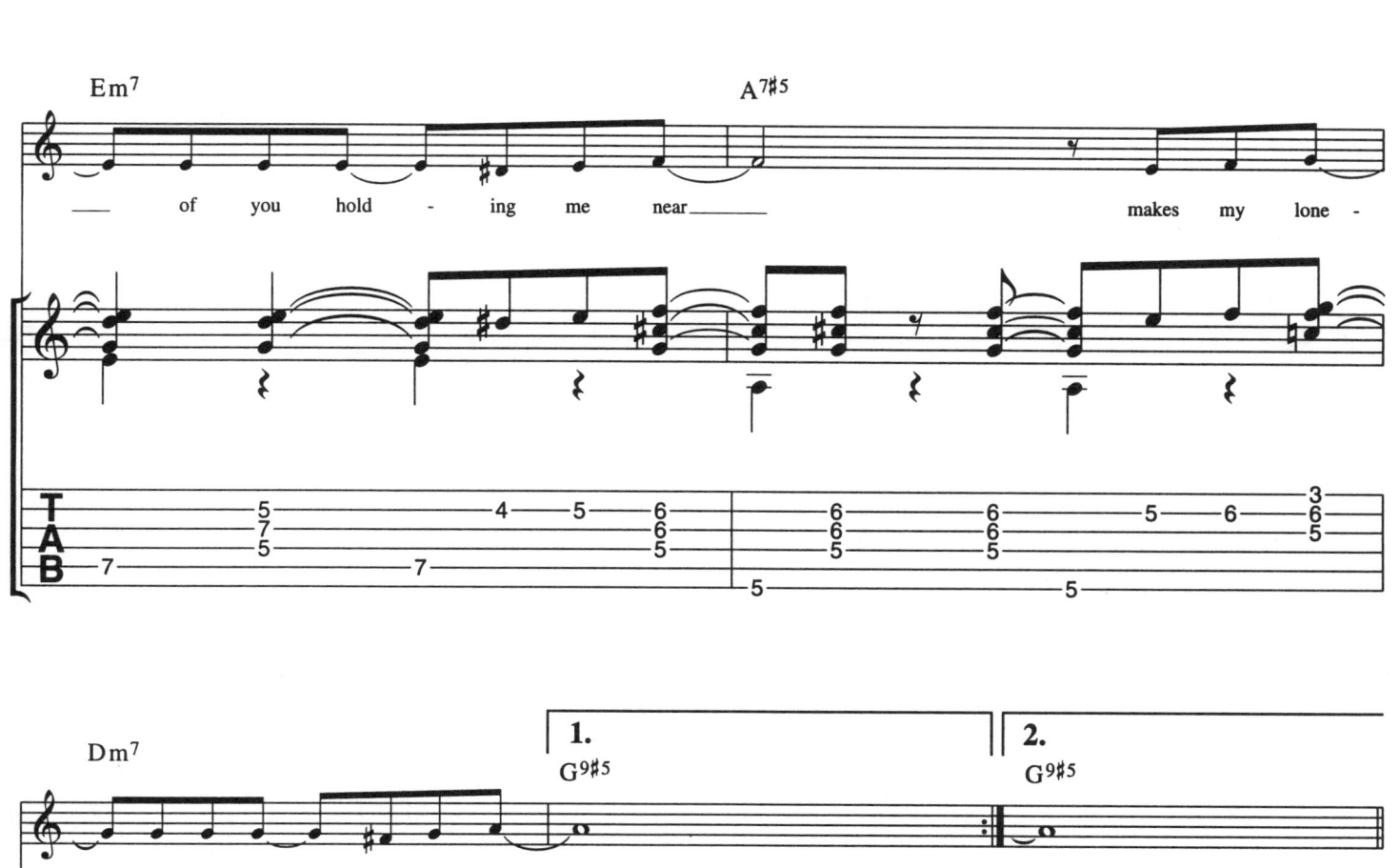

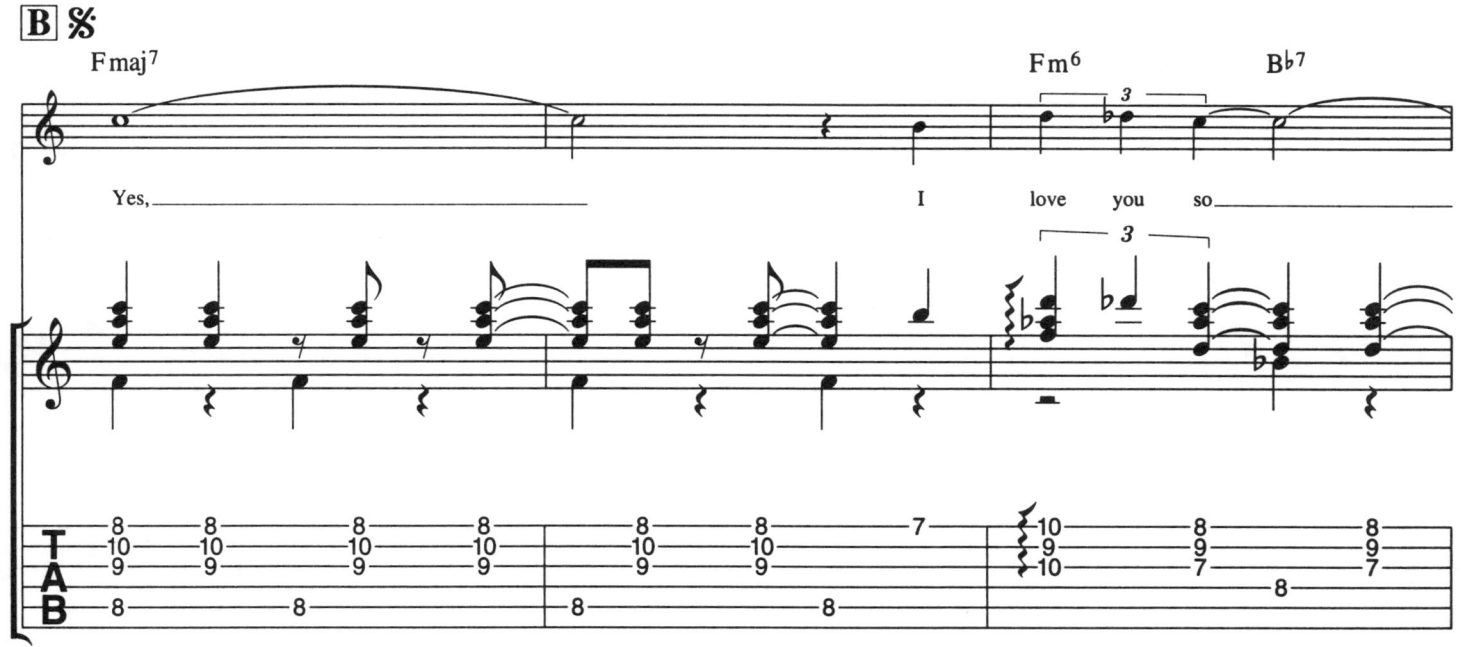

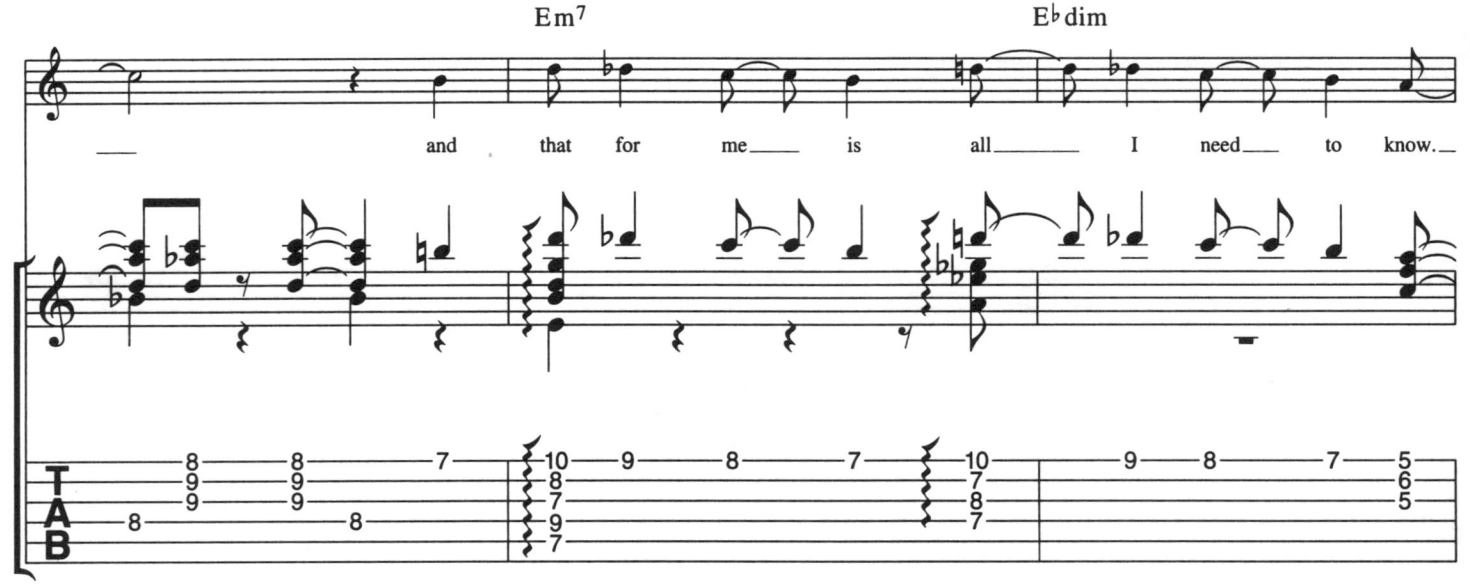
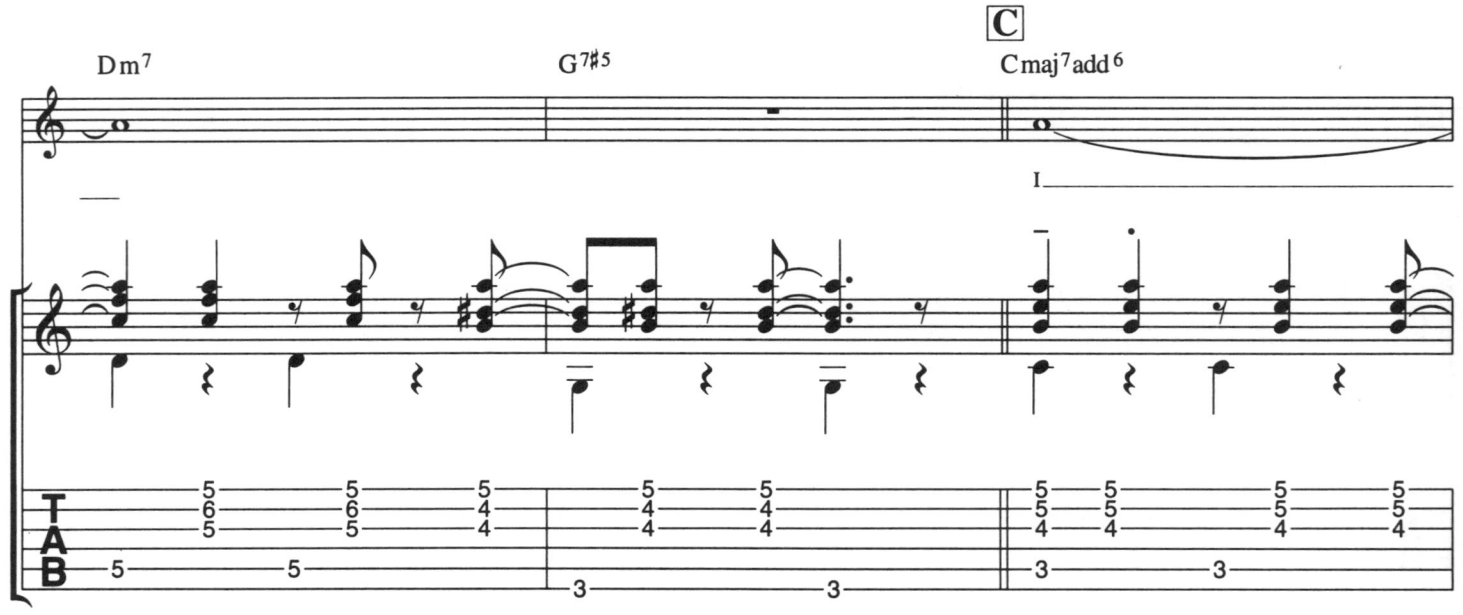
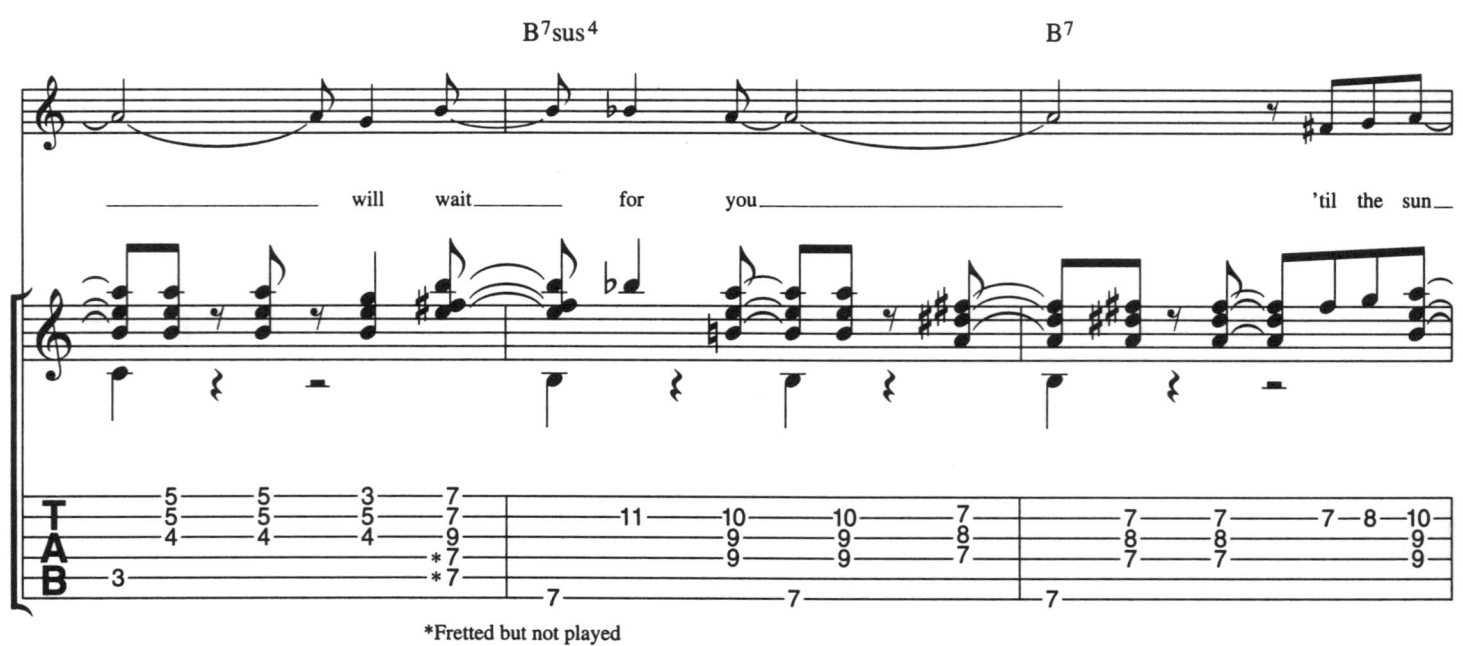

*Fretted but not played

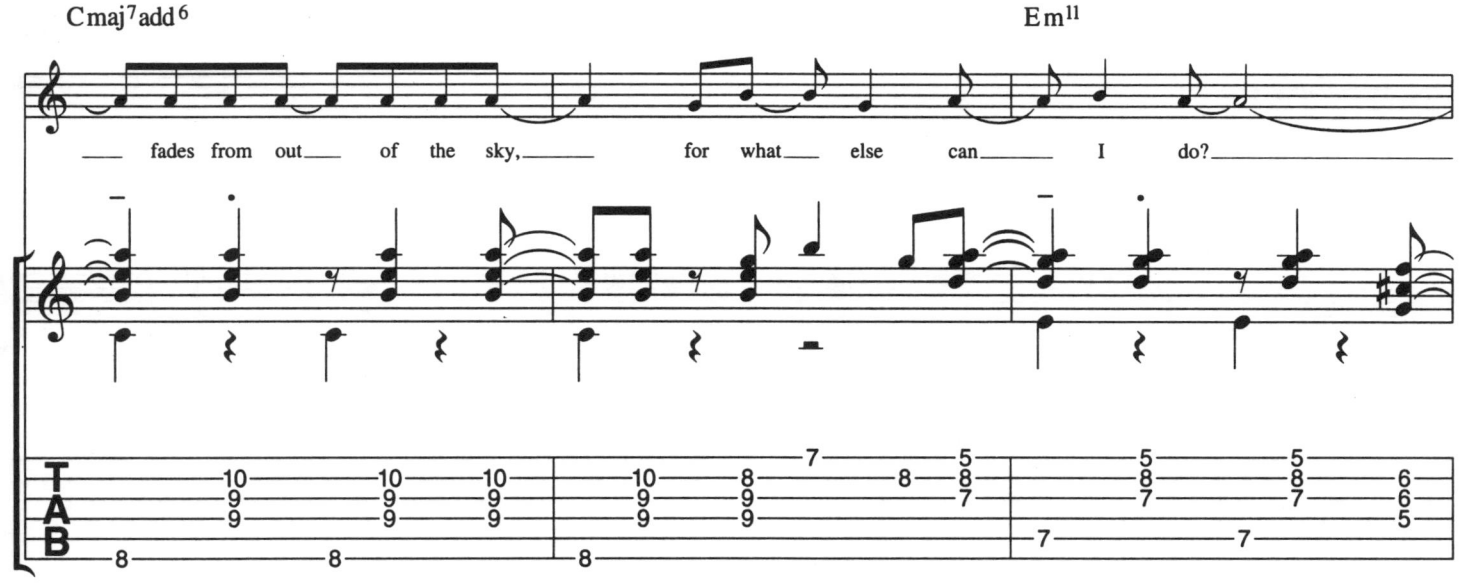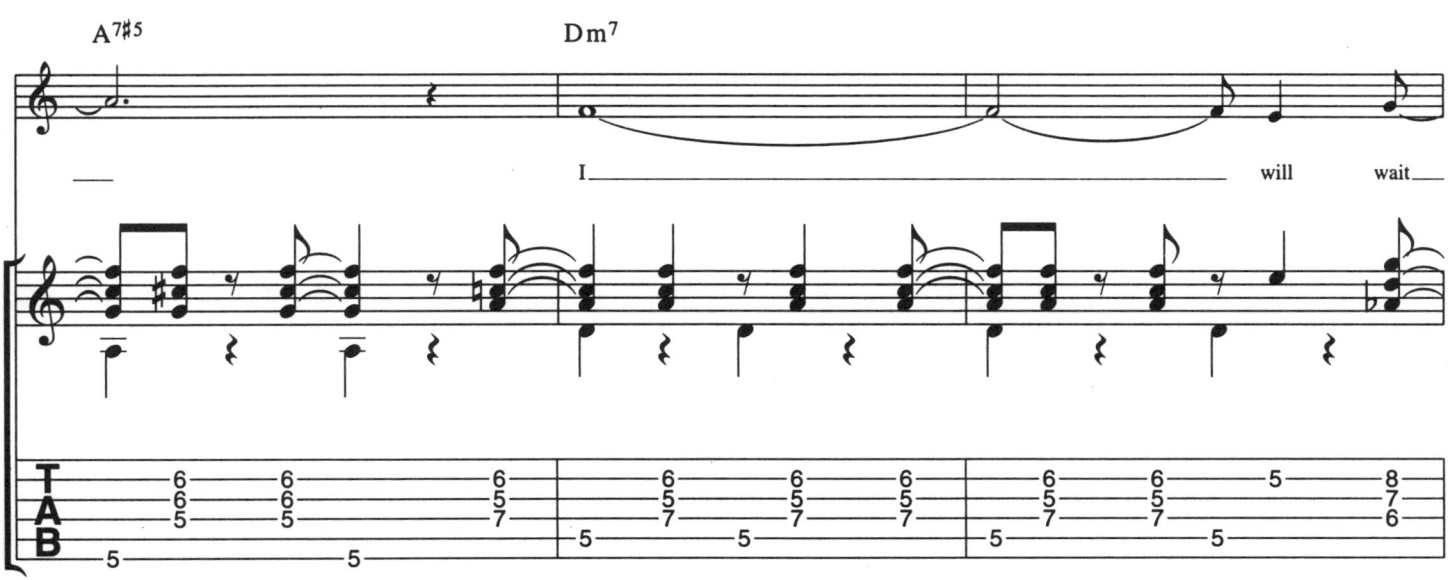

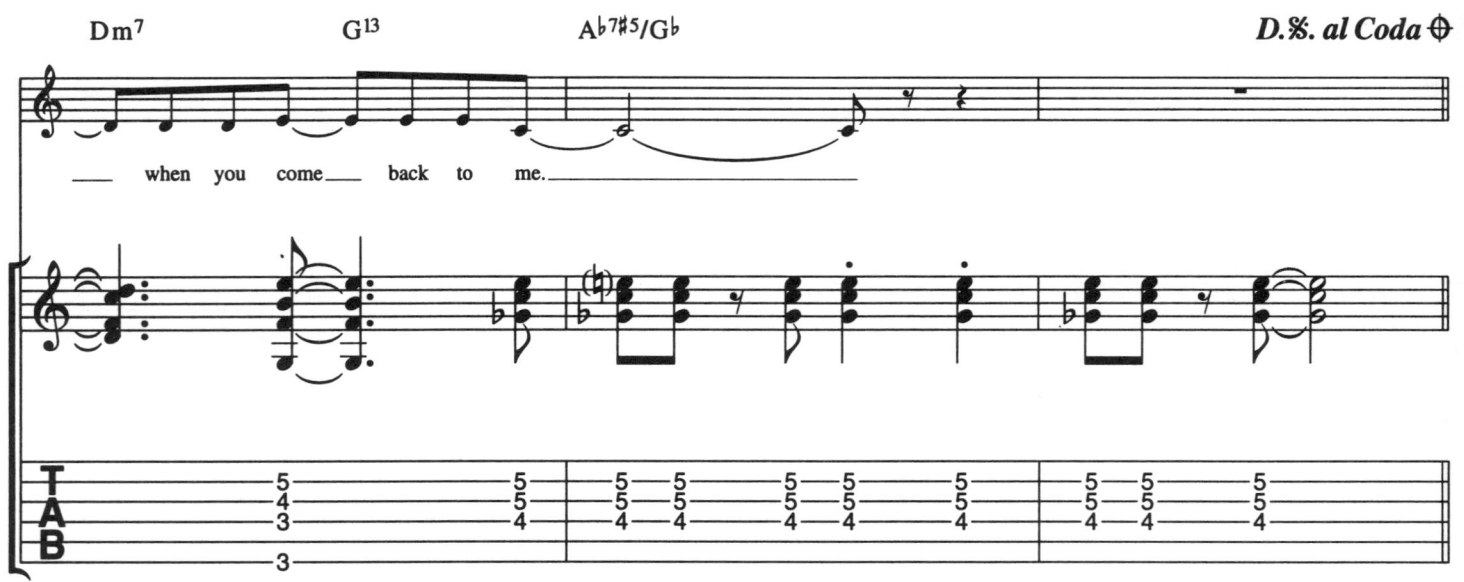
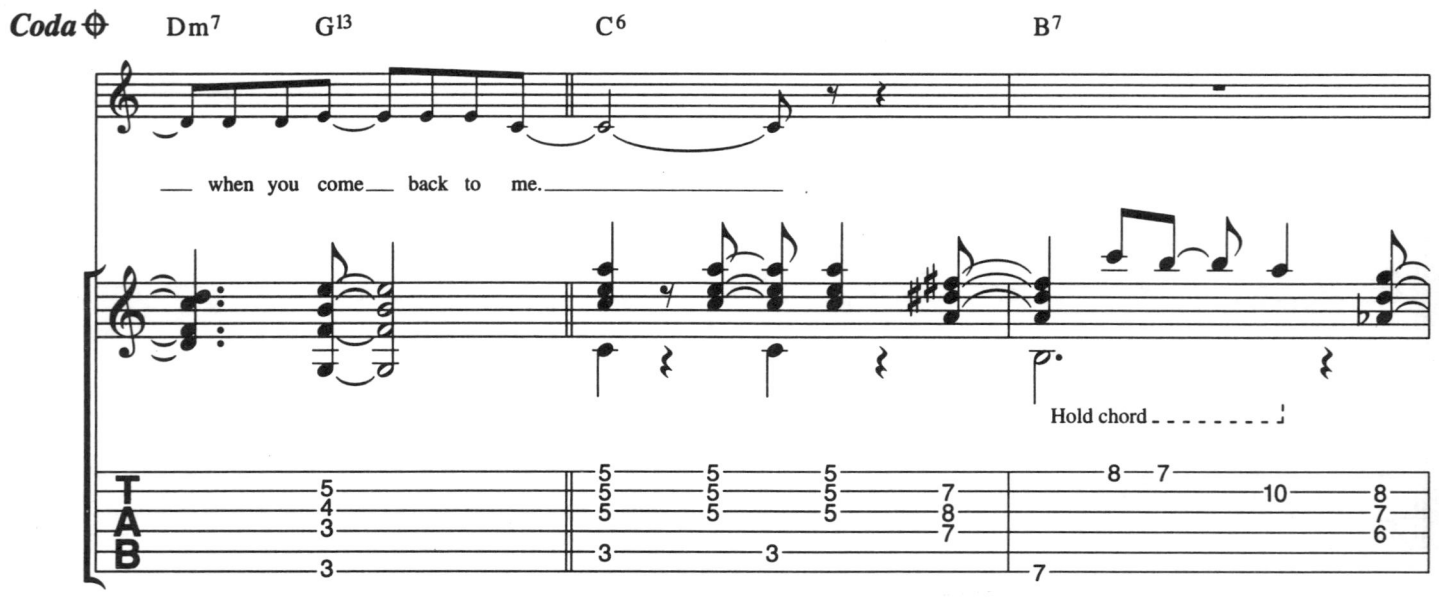
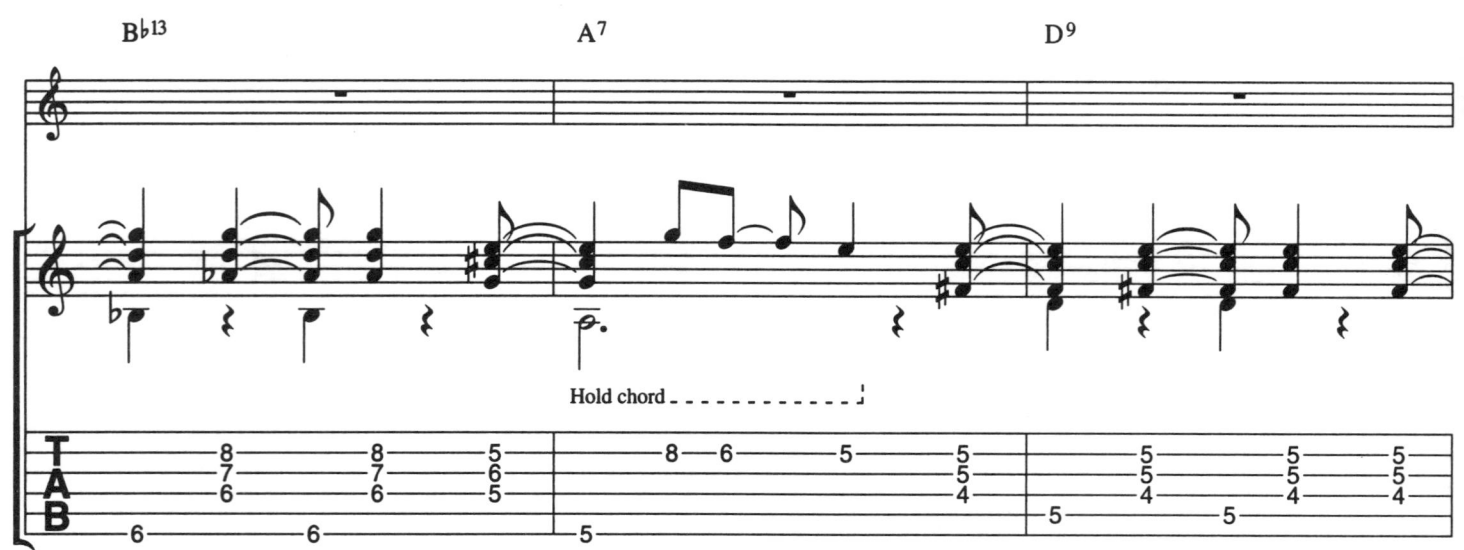

Verse 2:
Though you're far away
I have only to close my eyes and you are back to stay
I just close my eyes
And the sadness that missing you brings
Soon is gone and this heart of mine sings.

one note samba
(samba de uma nota so)

original words by n mendonca
english lyric by jon hendricks
music by antonio carlos jobim

The most effective way of playing this song is to make the chordal rhythm percussive. Try experimenting with the feel making some notes long and some notes short. At **B** the guitar part can follow the vocal line or continue as a rhythm accompaniment.

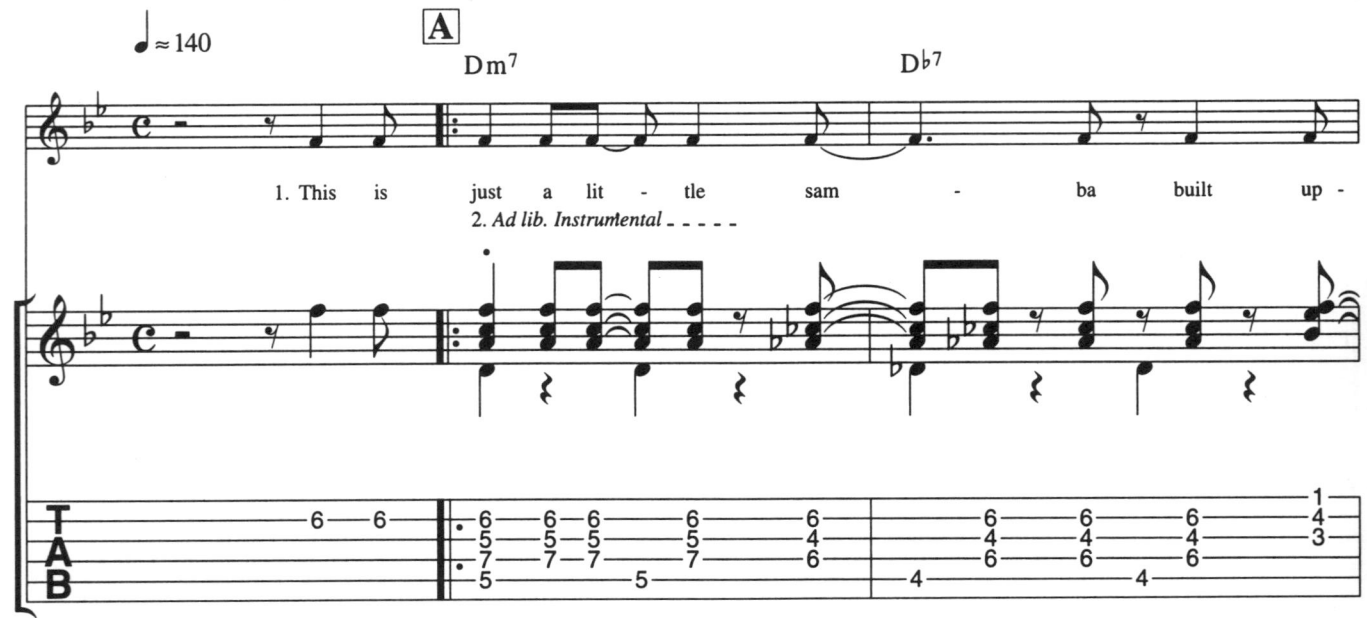

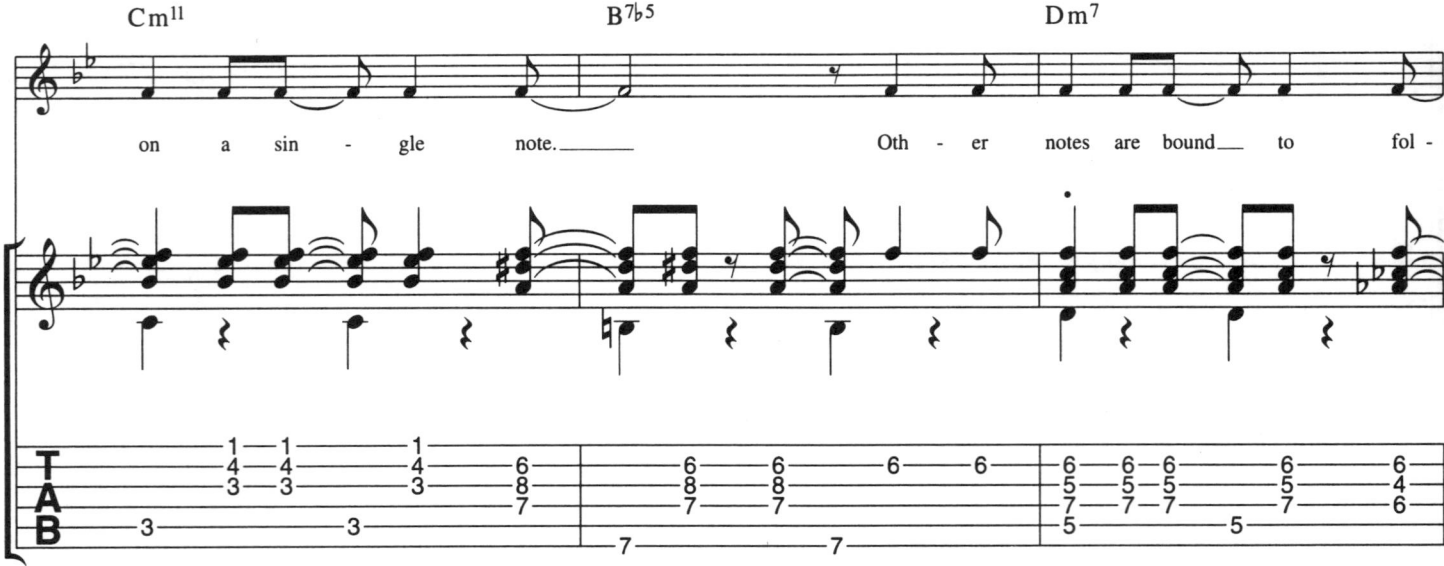

© copyright 1961, 1962, 1964 antonio carlos jobim and mrs n mendonca, brazil
mca music limited, 77 fulham palace road, london w6 for the british commonwealth (excluding canada)
all rights reserved
international copyright secured

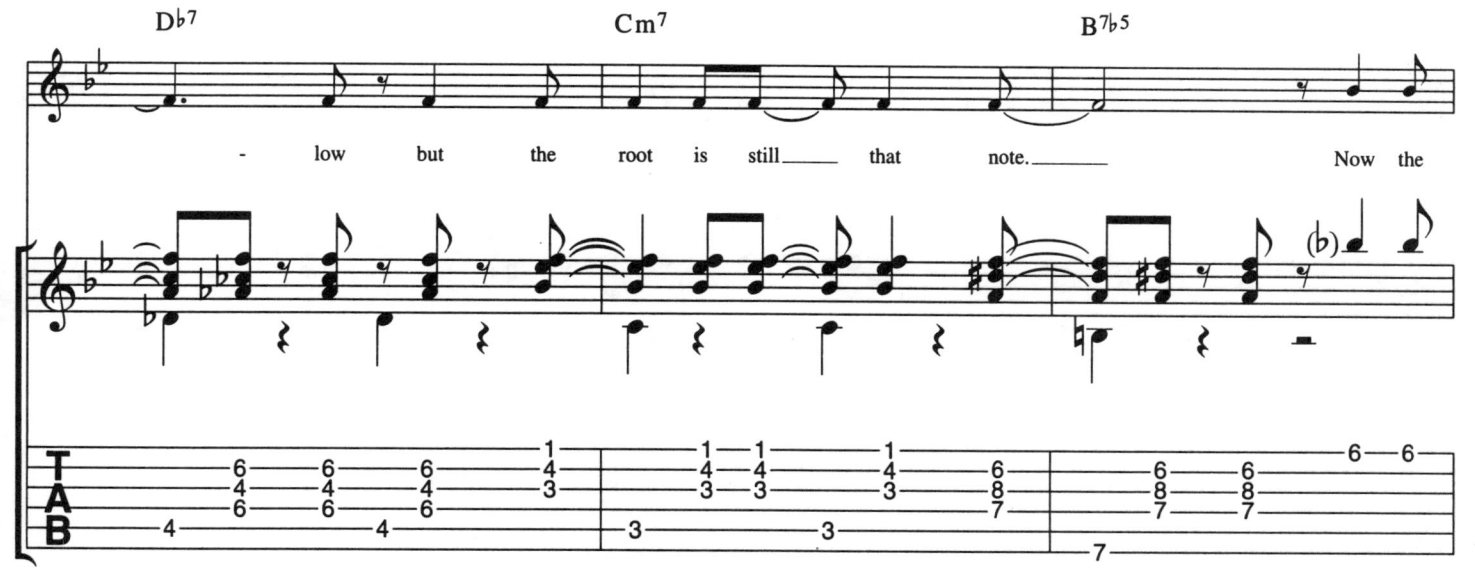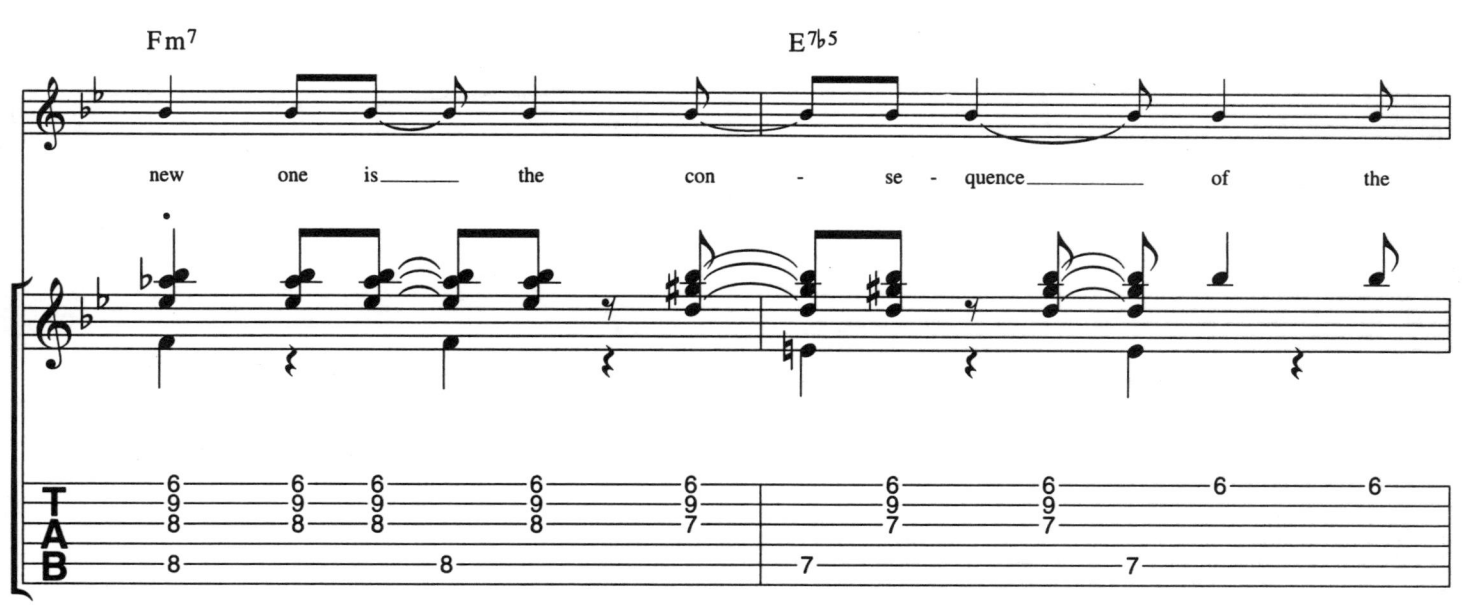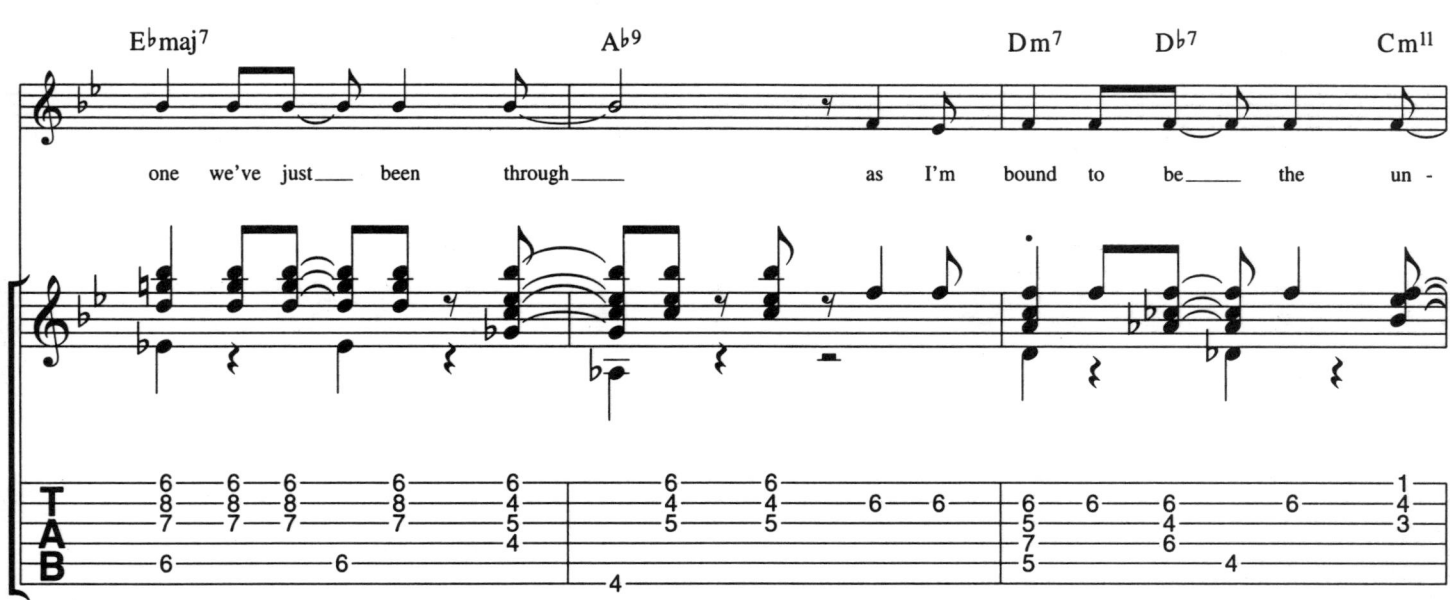

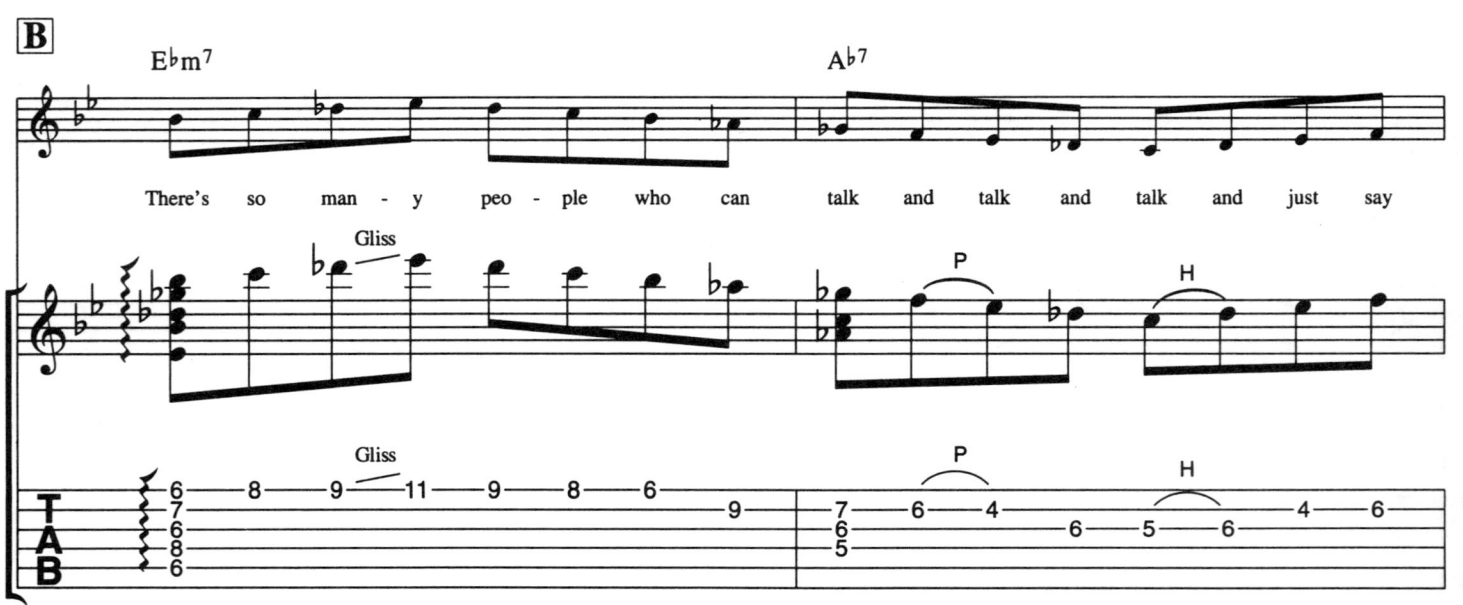

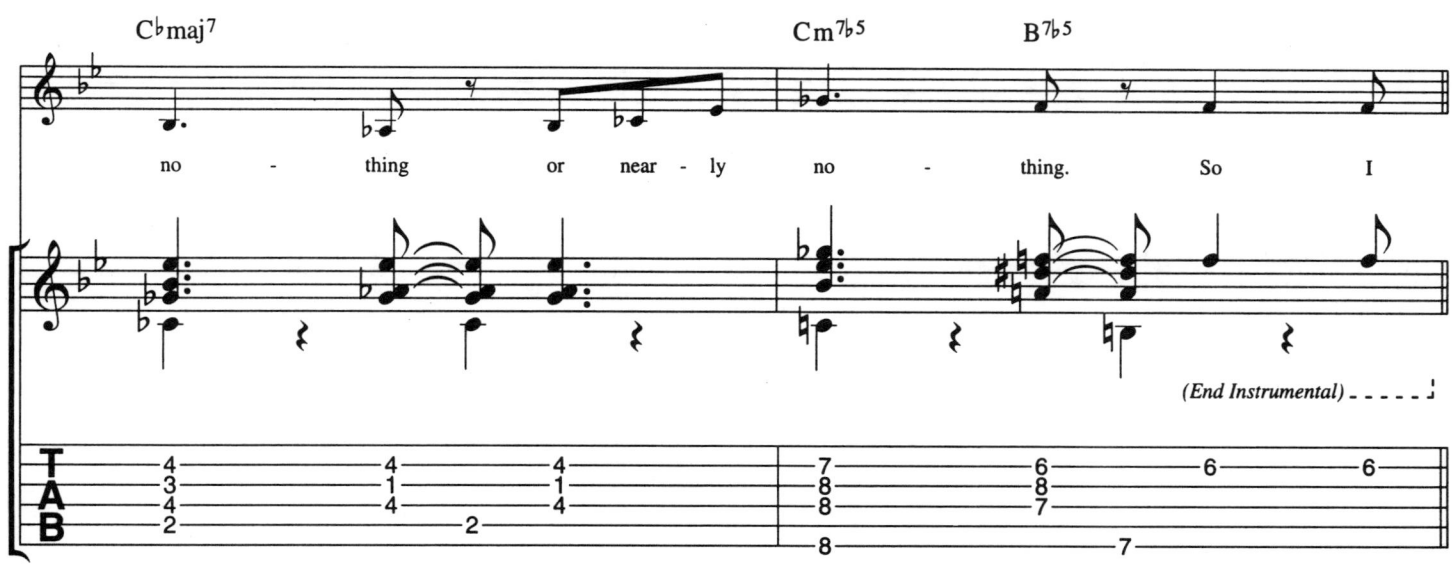
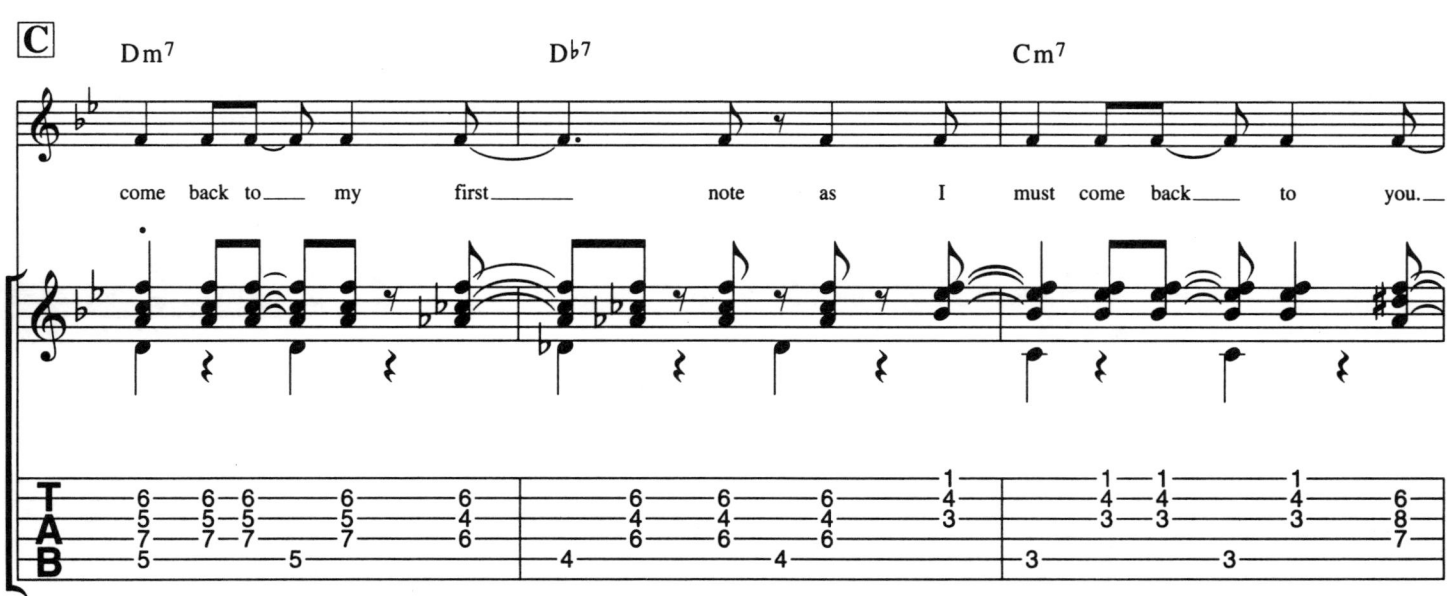

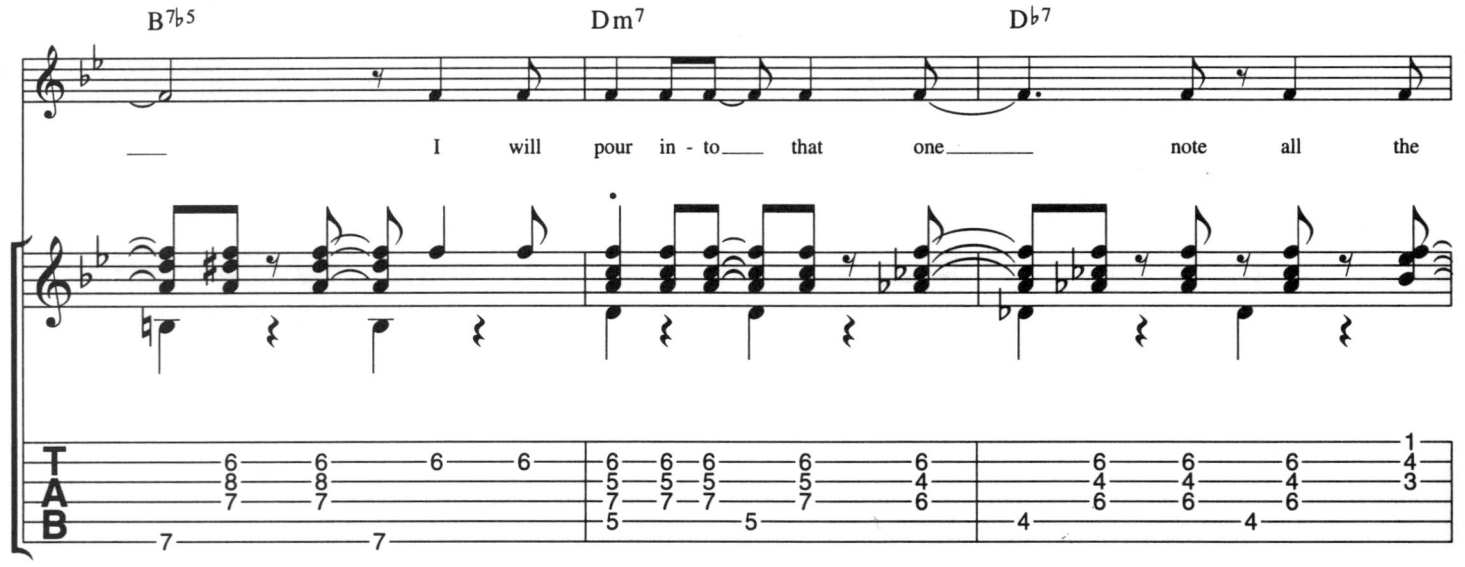

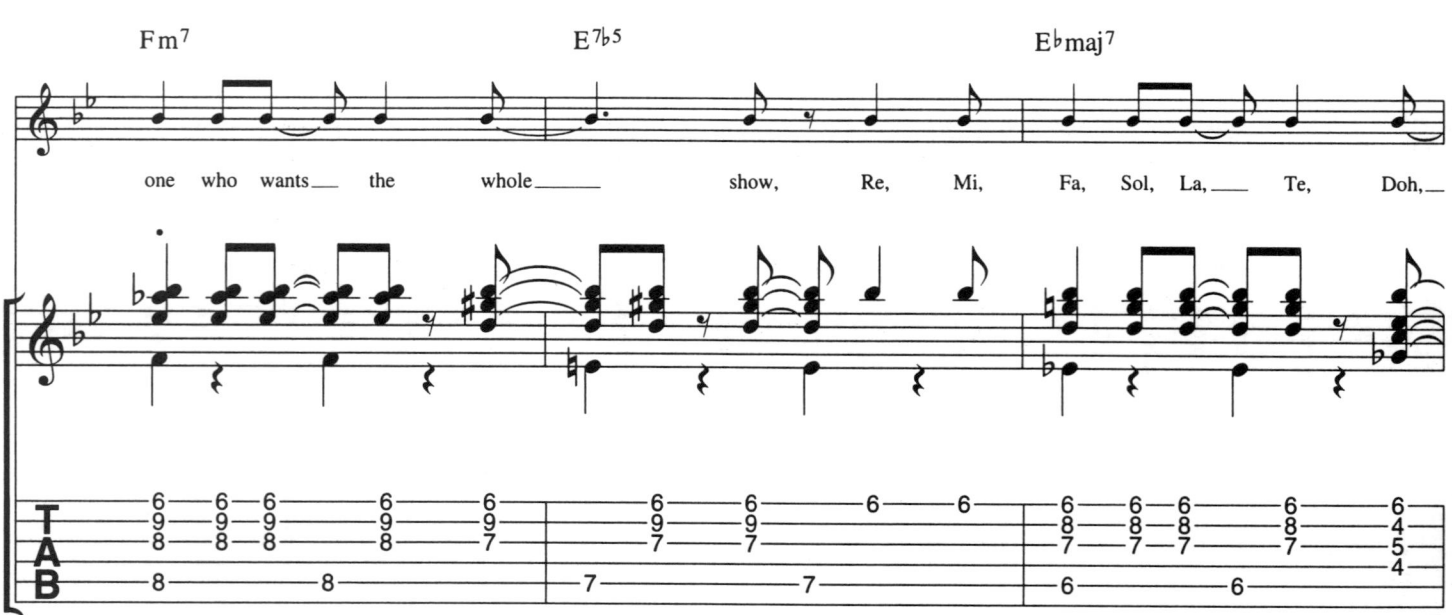

36

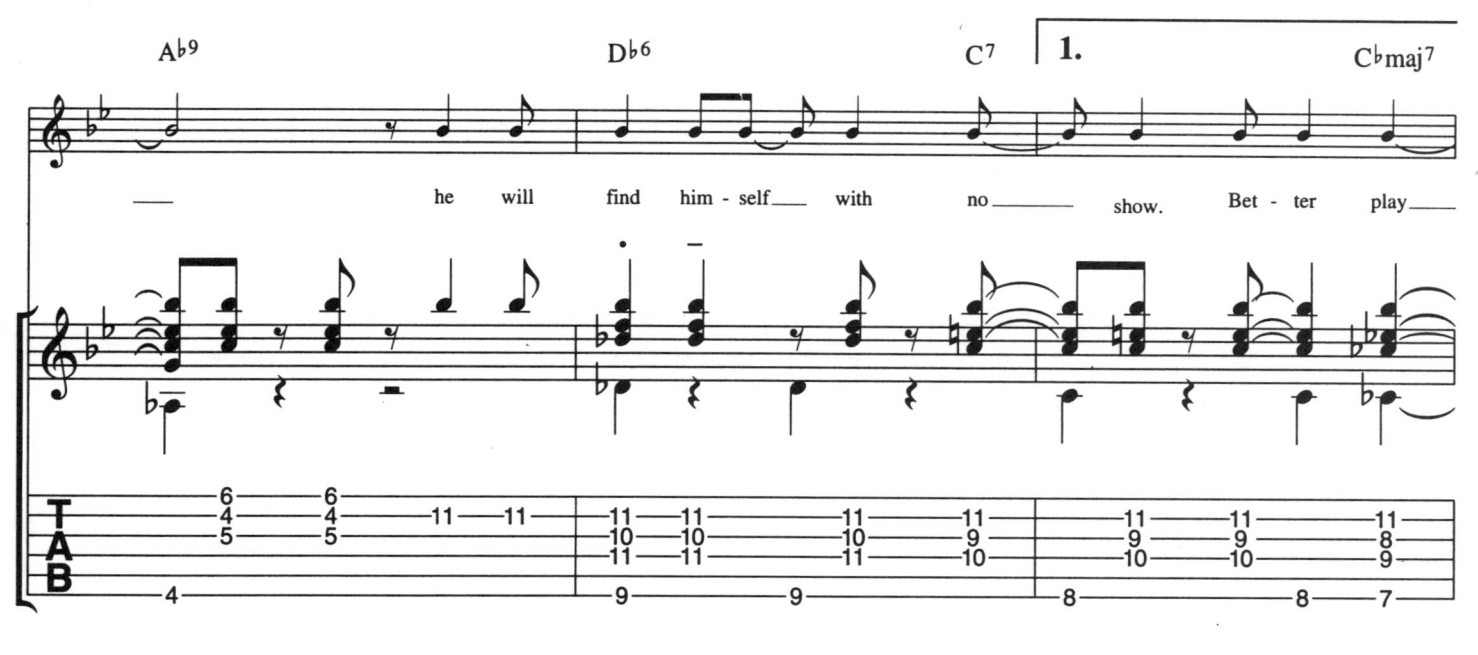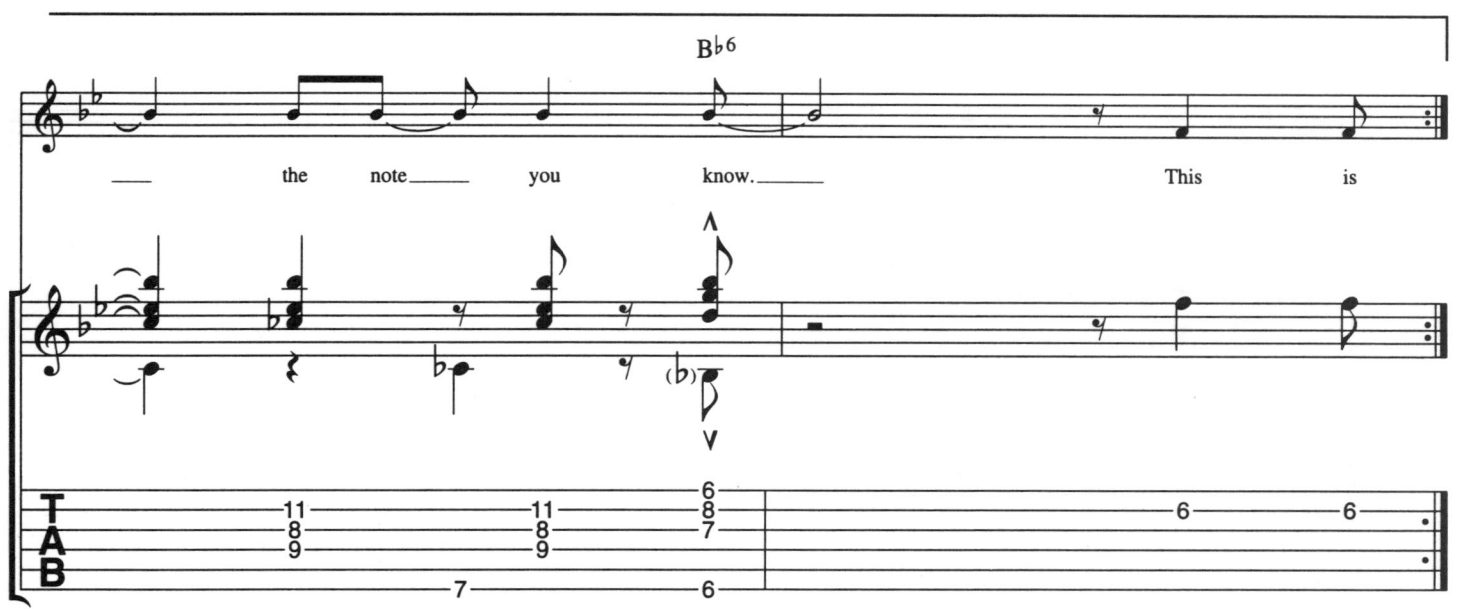

somewhere in the hills
(o morro nao tem vez (favela))

music & original words by antonio carlos jobim & vinicius de moraes
english lyric by ray gilbert

Favela means music written for a play. In this piece it describes the slums which lie in the hills around the city of Rio. The guitar plays a simple accompaniment to this haunting melody, which can either be sung, or played on the flute.

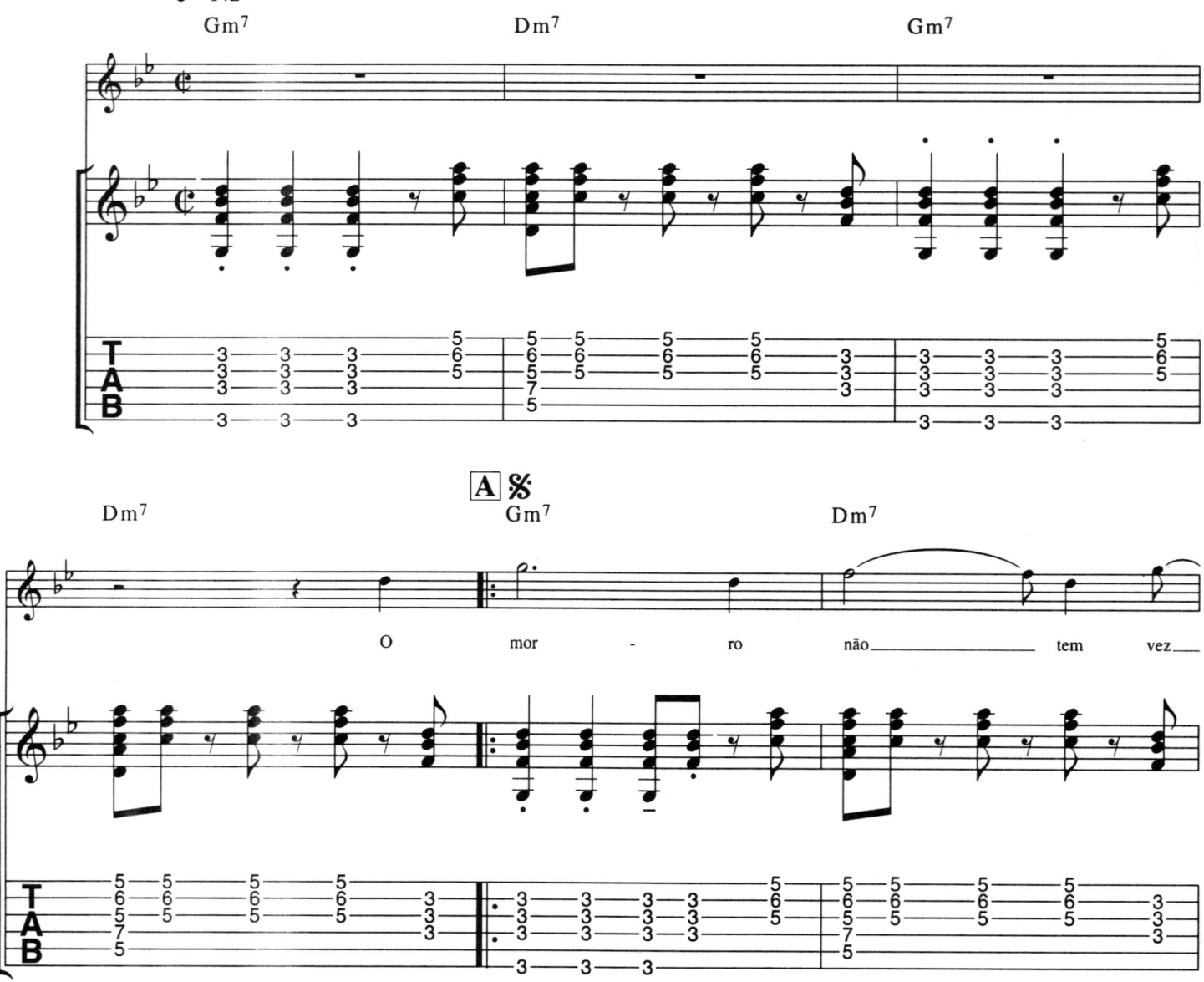

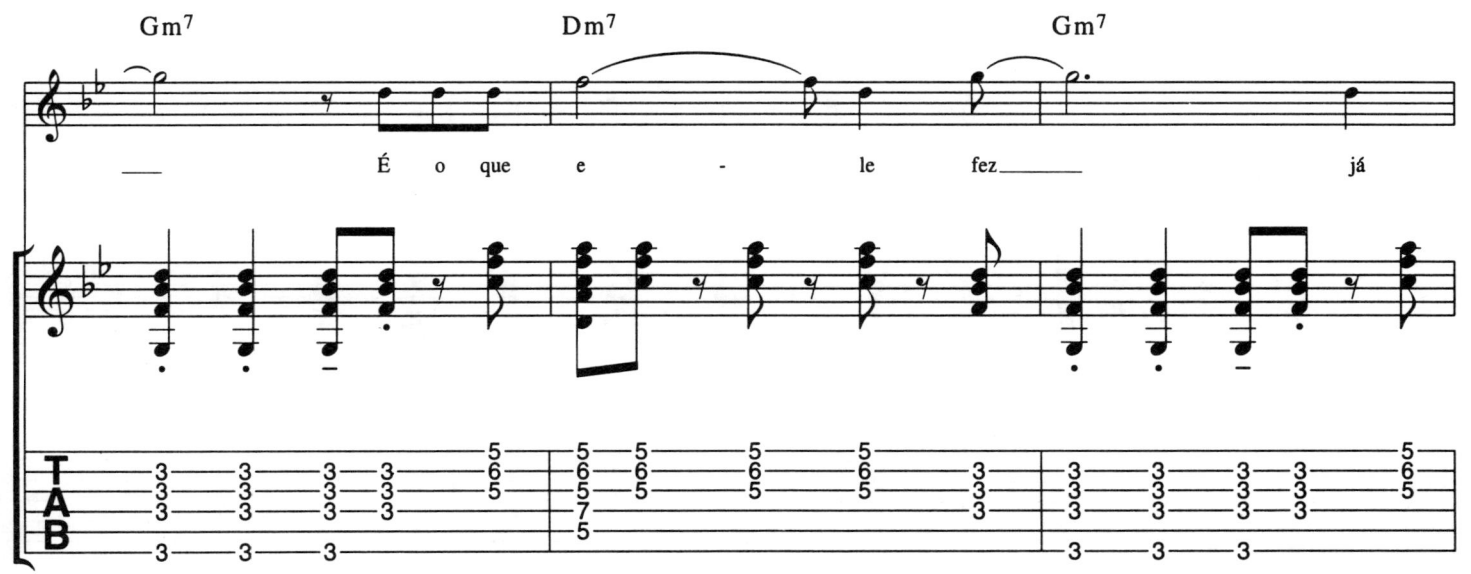
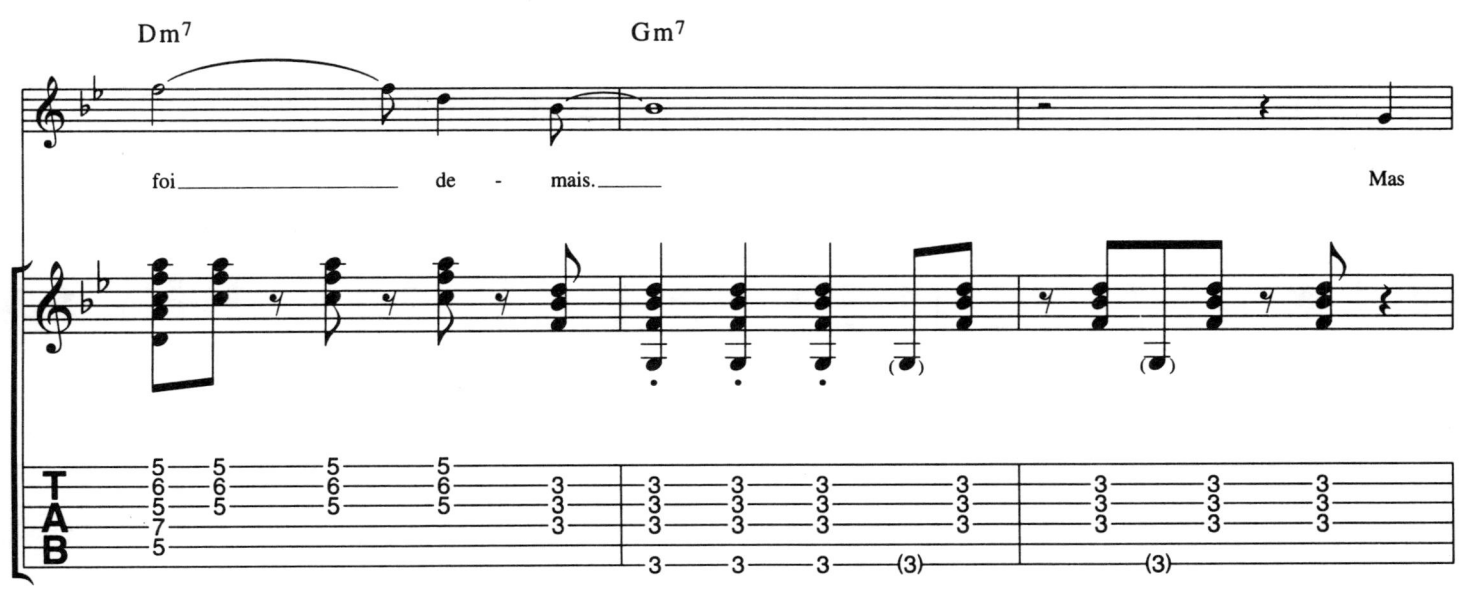
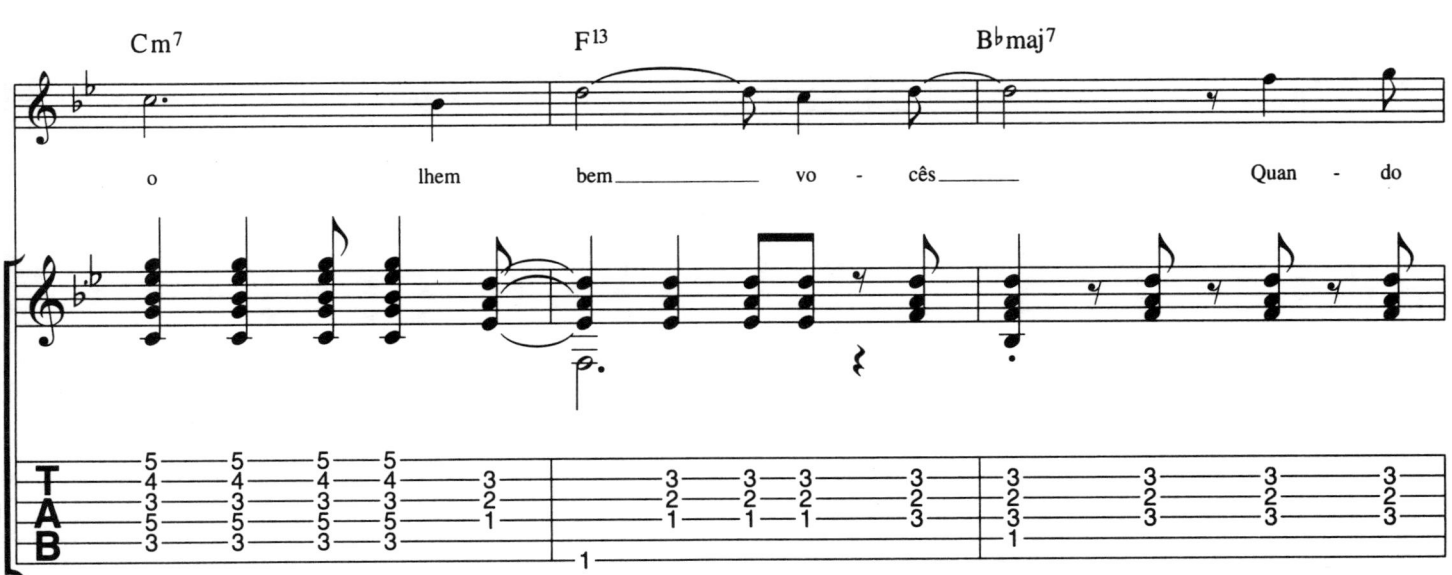

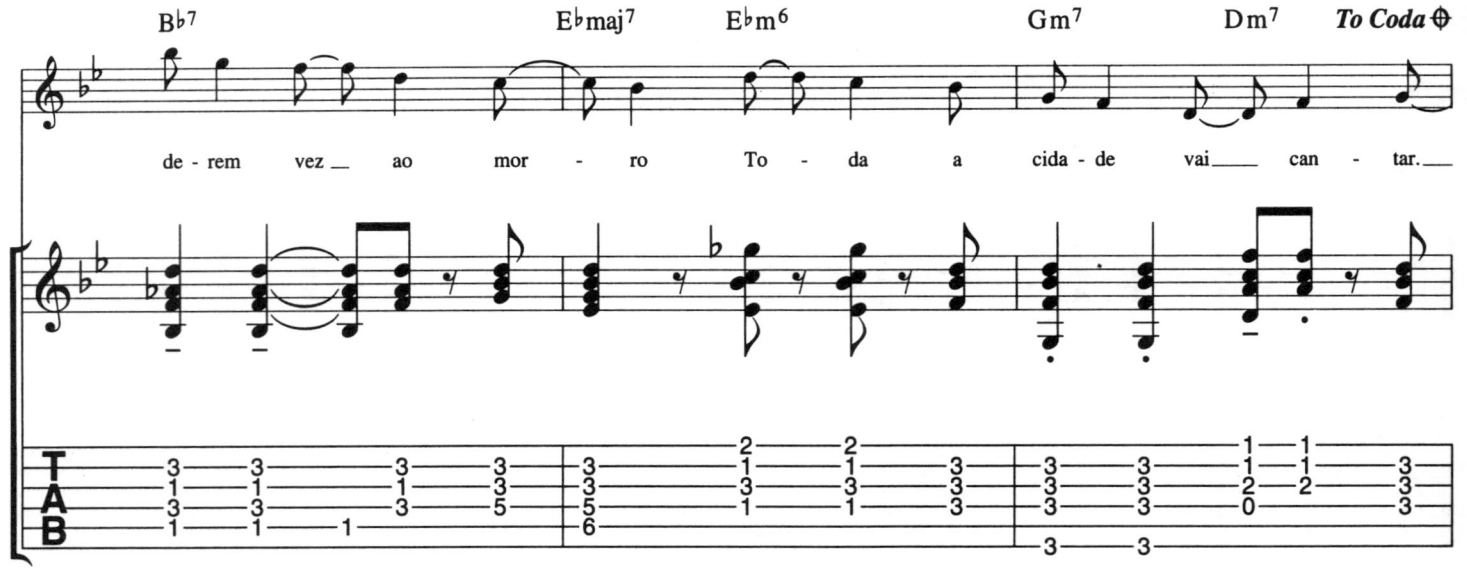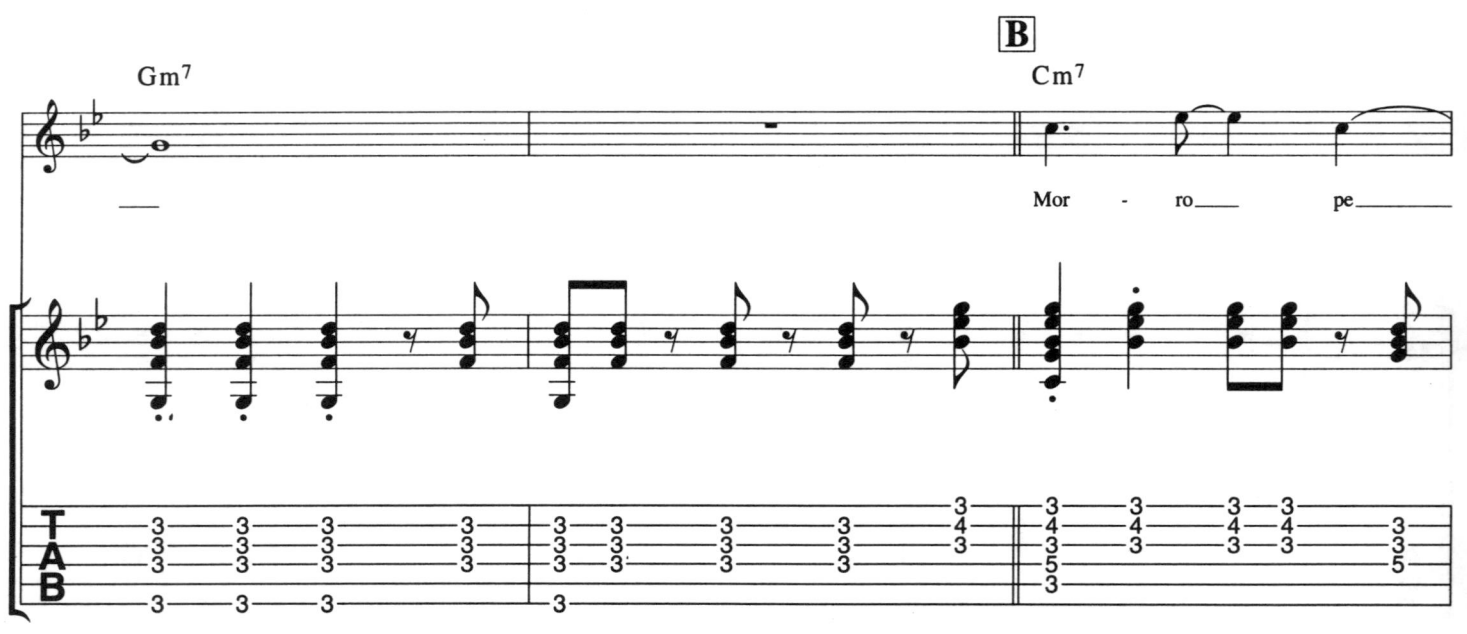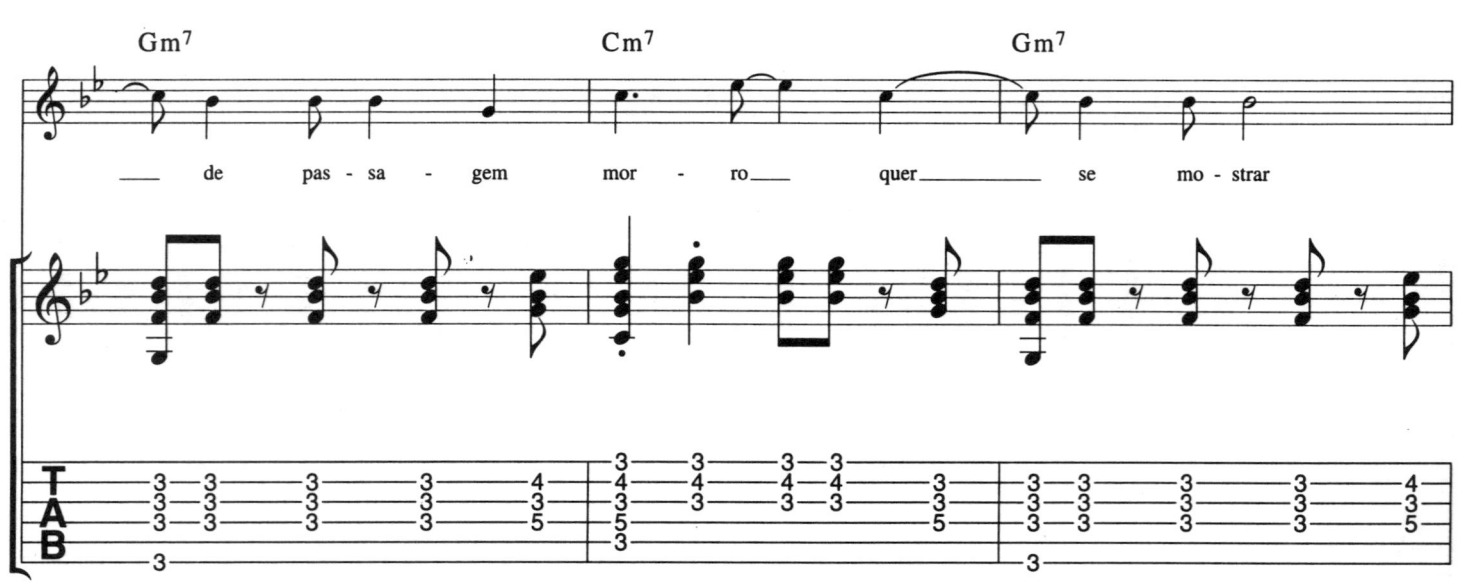

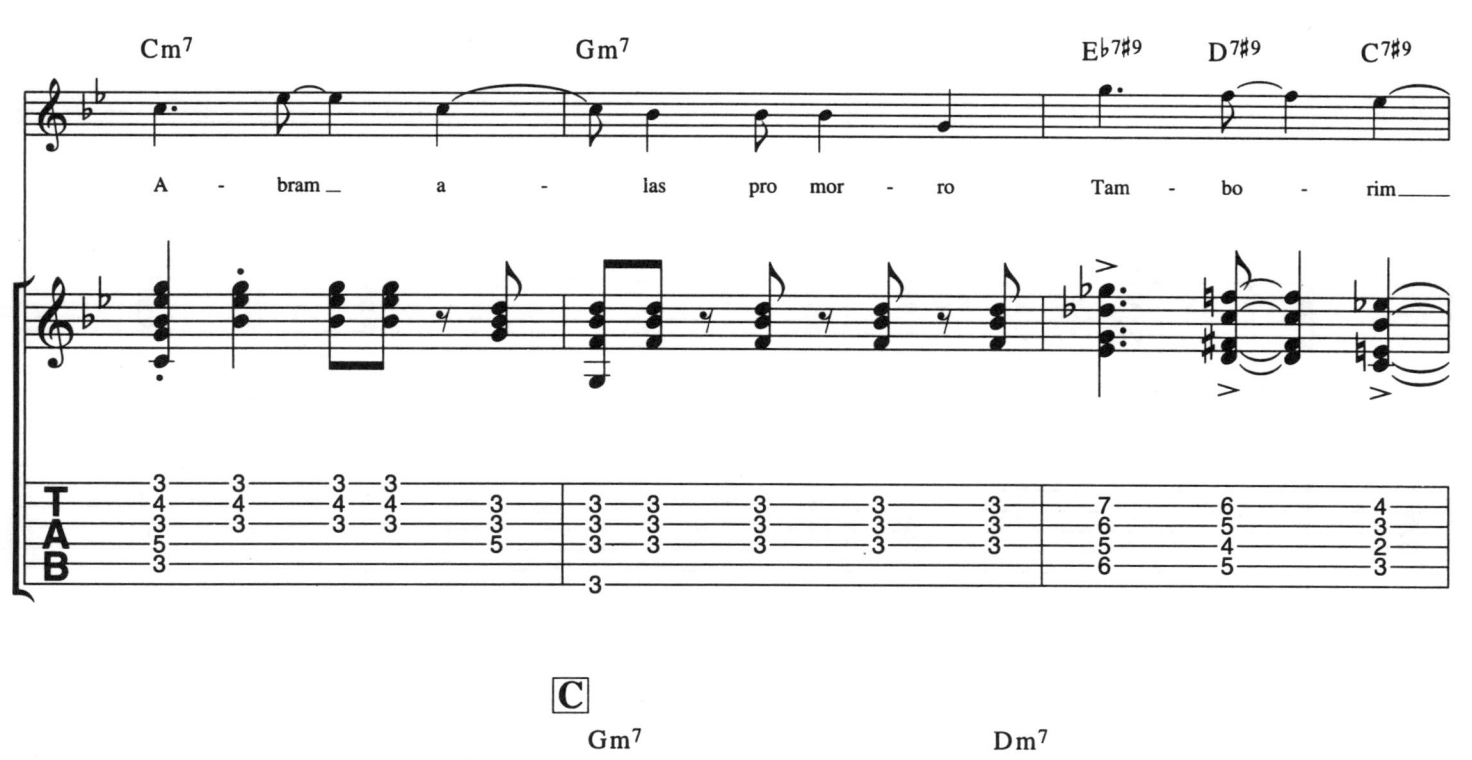
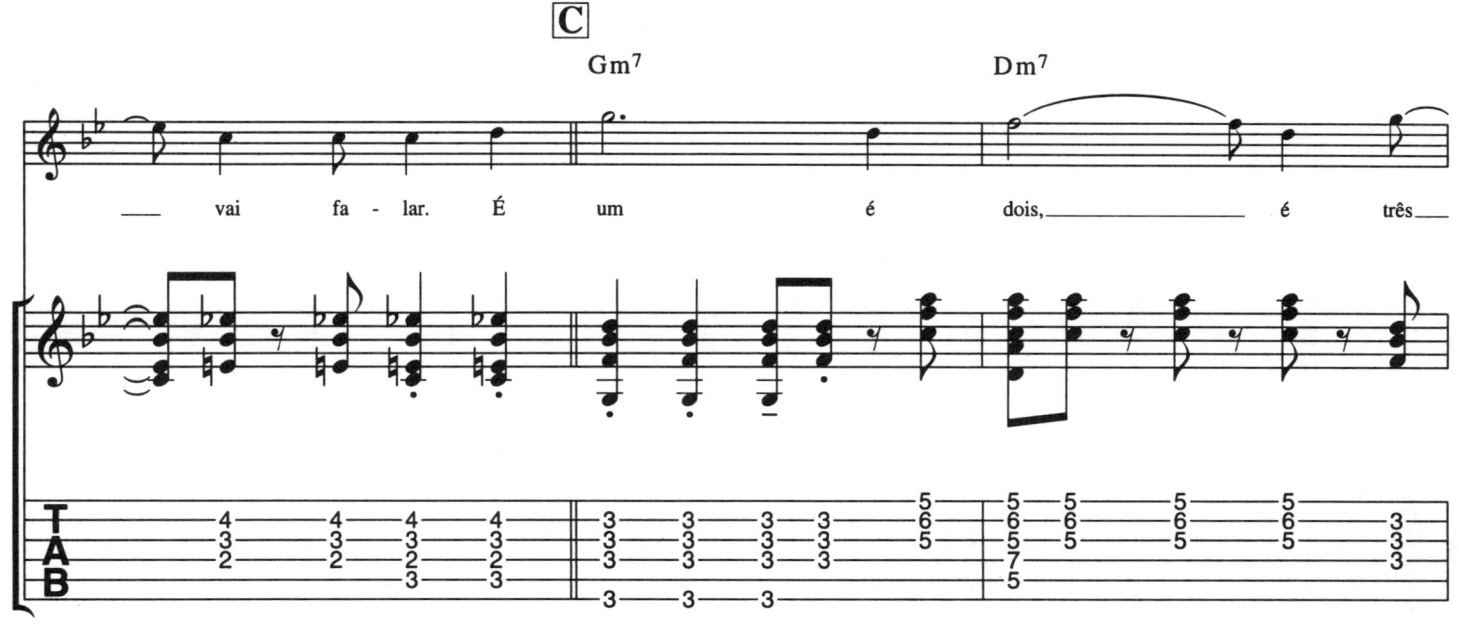
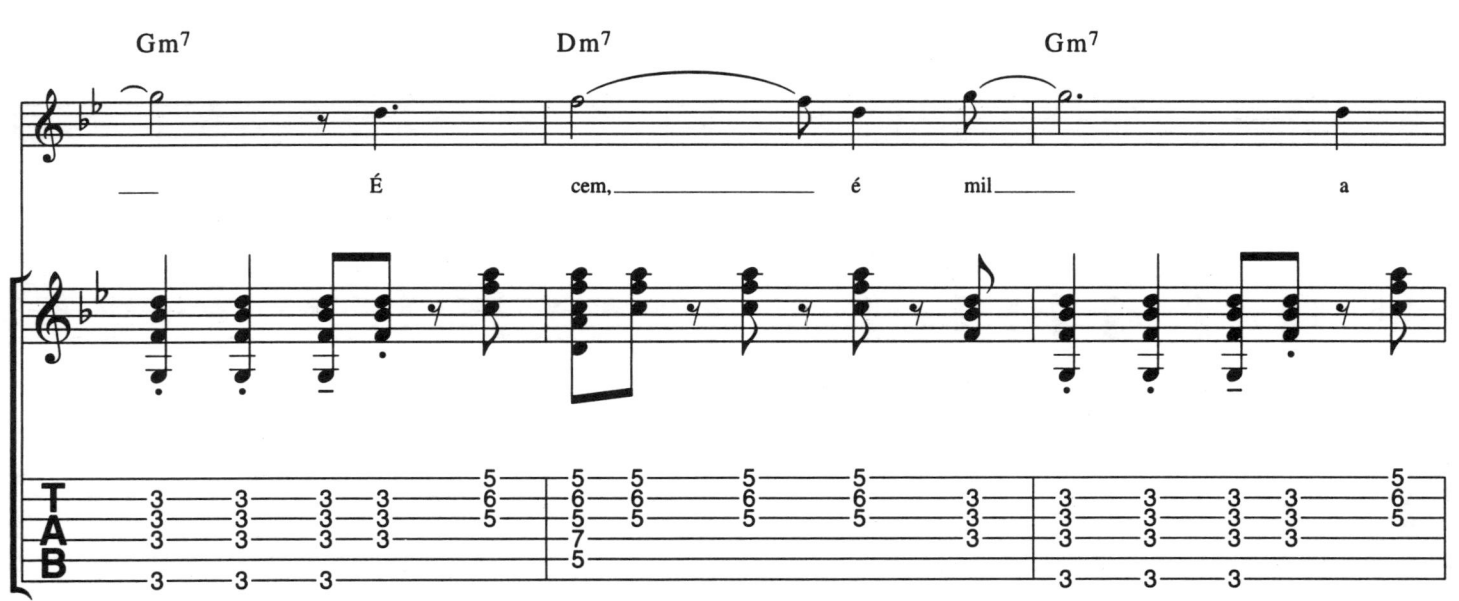

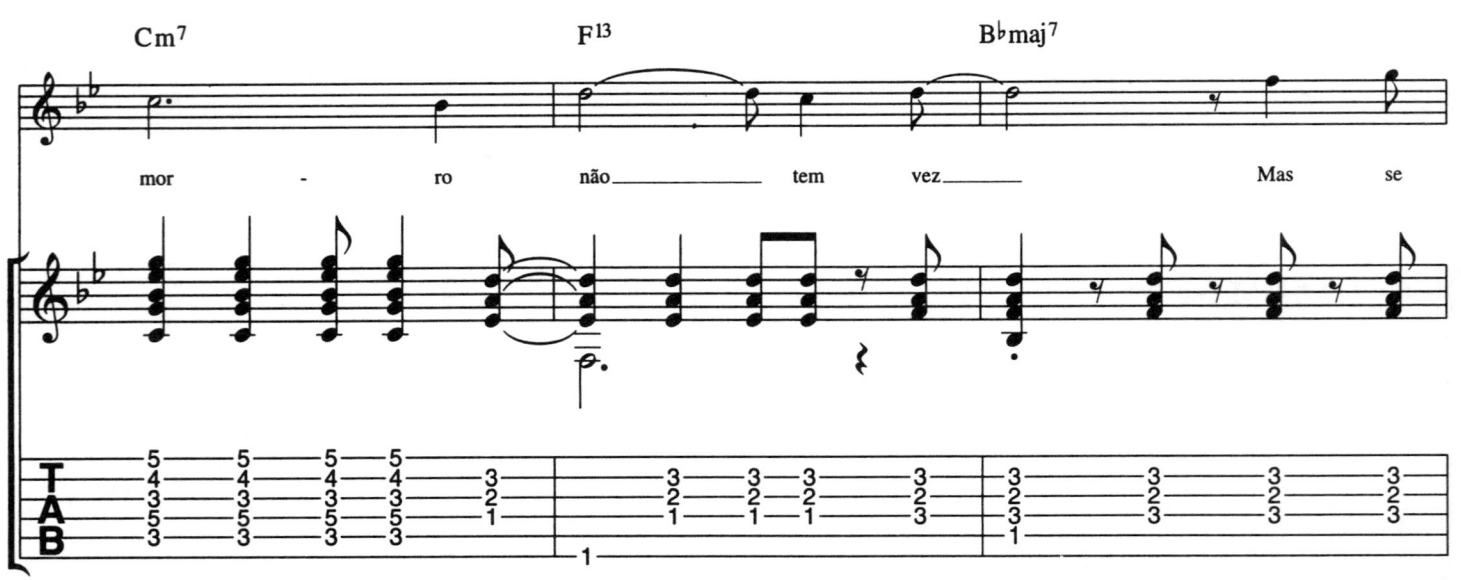
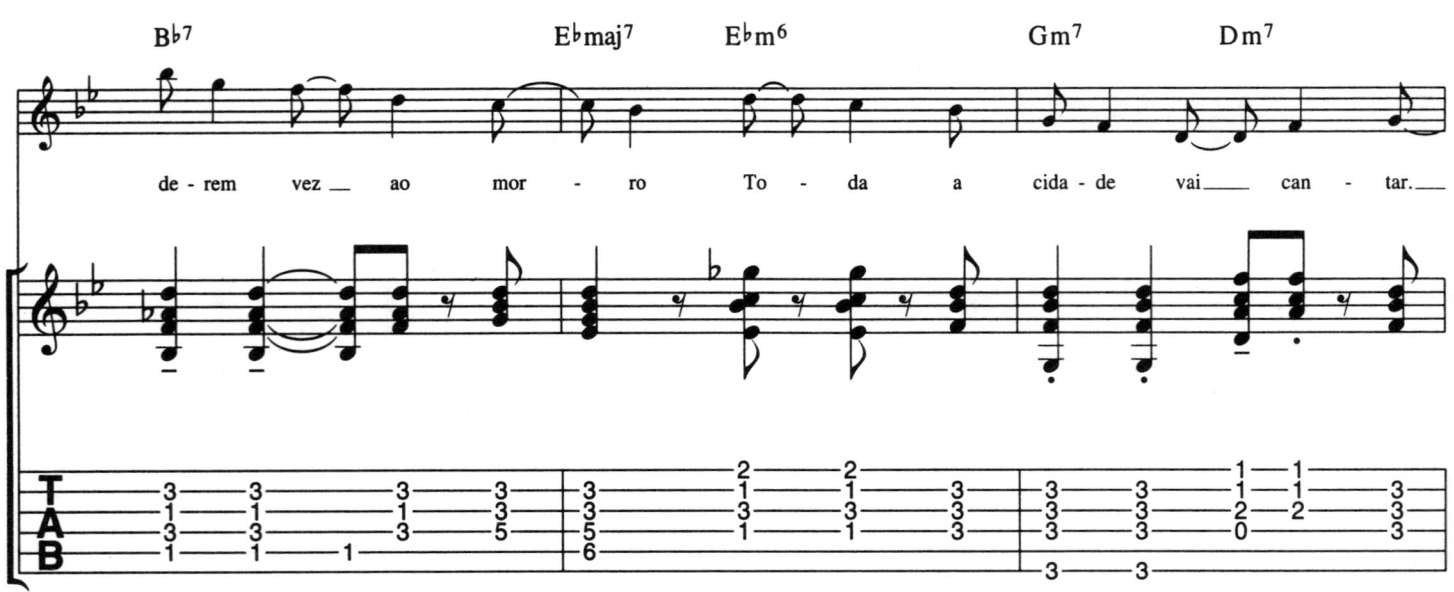

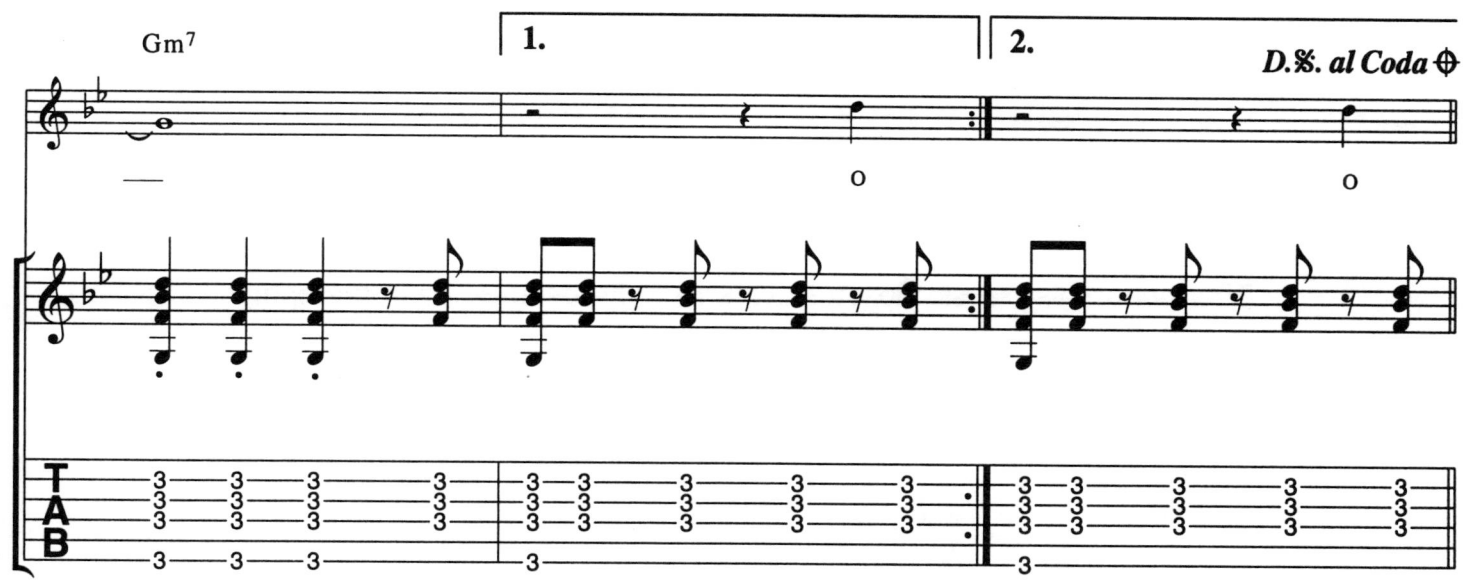
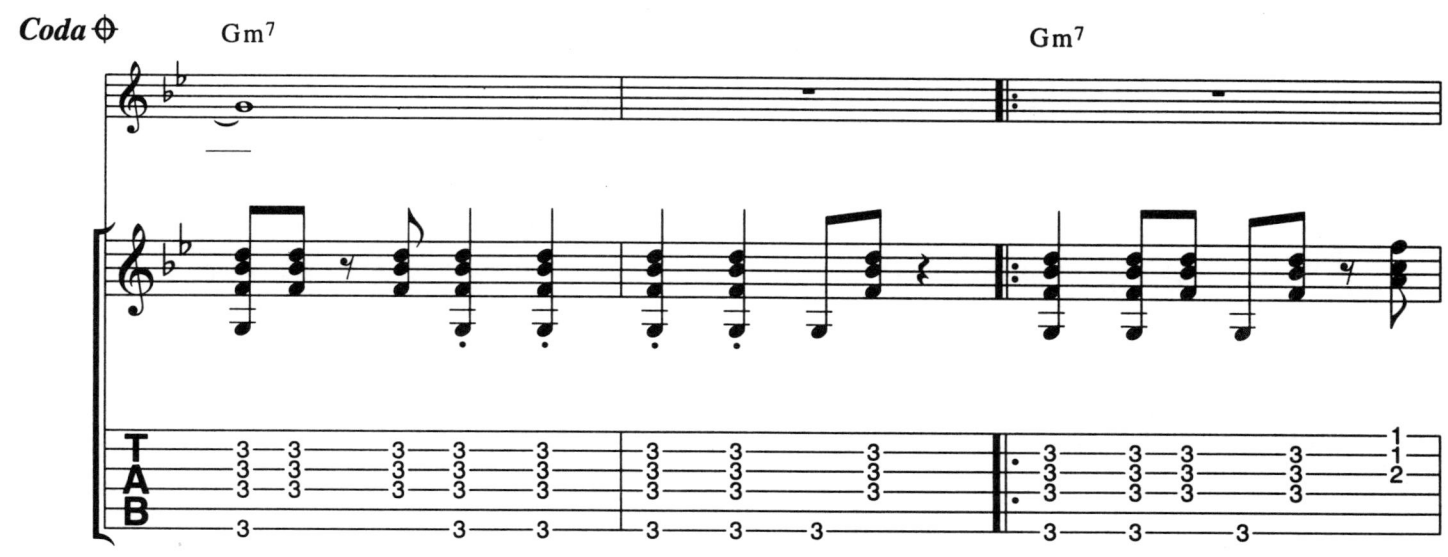
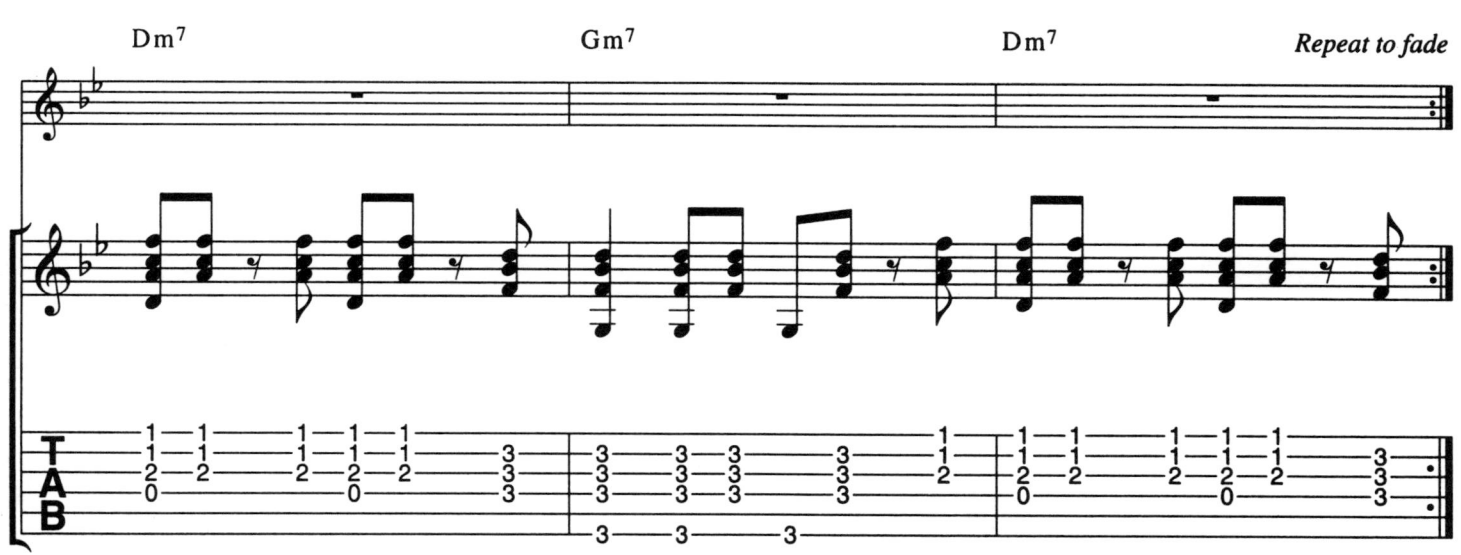

the girl from ipanema
(garota de ipanema)

original words by vinicius de moraes
english lyric by norman gimbel
music by antonio carlos jobim

The feel of this classic Bossa Nova should be established in the opening four bars. Use a mixture of strumming and fingerstyle and try to keep the tempo even throughout the piece. Ipanema is the name given to a sand spit between the lagoon and sea next to Copacabana beach.

© copyright 1963 antonio carlos jobim and vinicius de moraes, brazil
mca music limited, 77 fulham palace road, london w6 for the british commonwealth
(excluding canada) south africa, eire, germany, austria, switzerland, france and italy
all rights reserved
international copyright secured

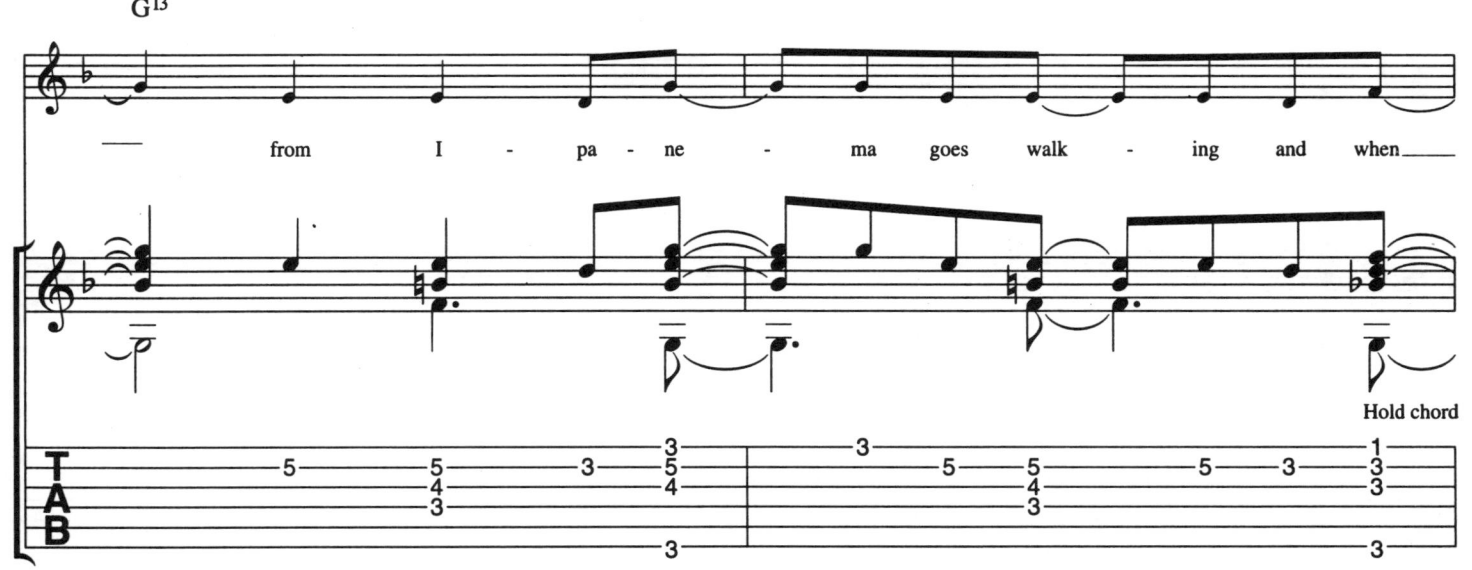
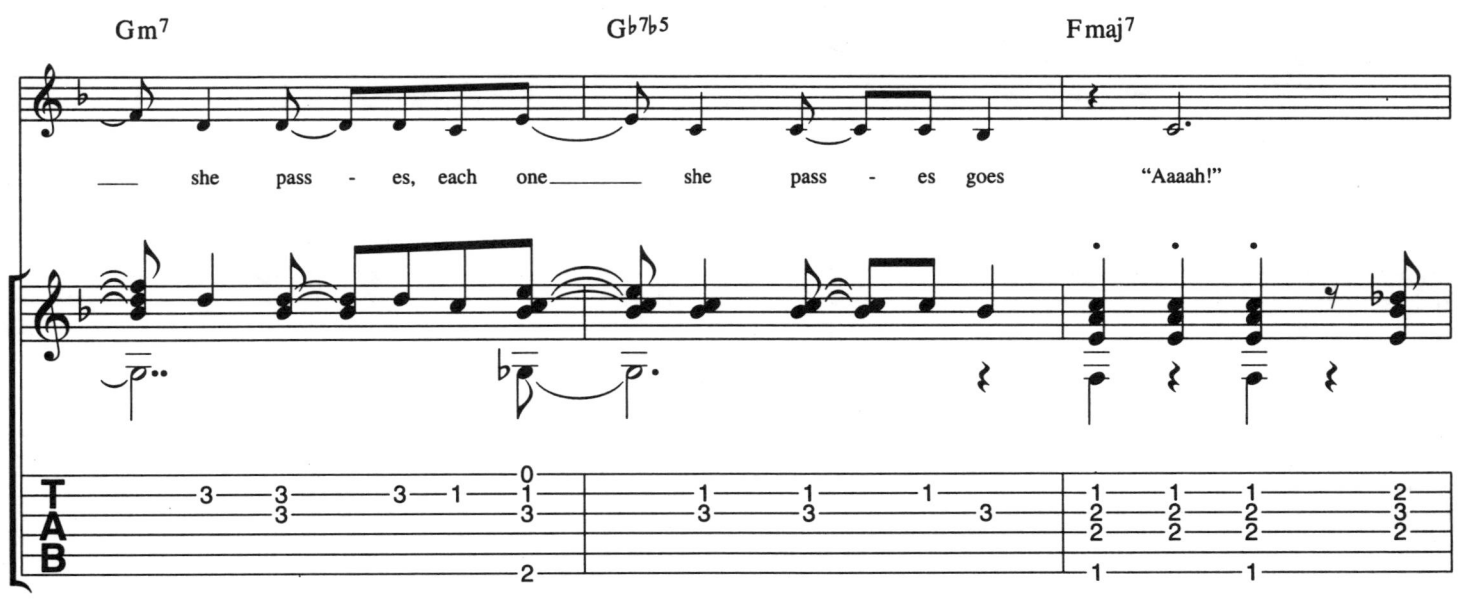
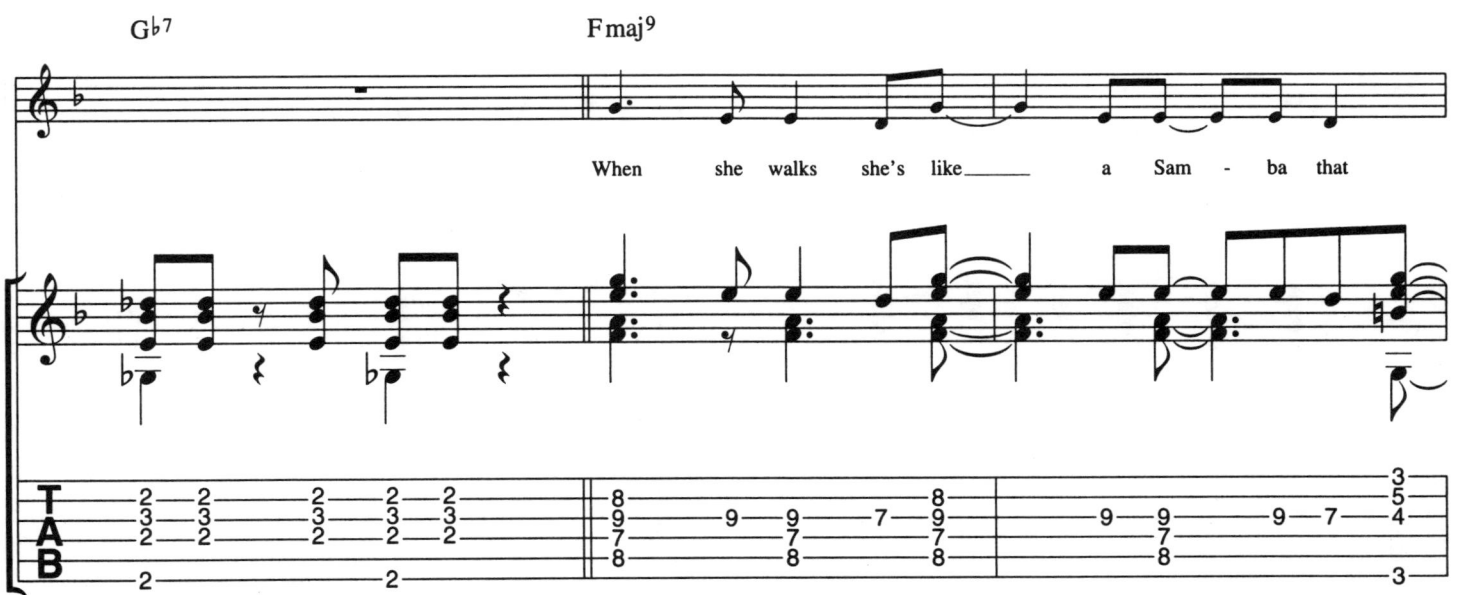

45

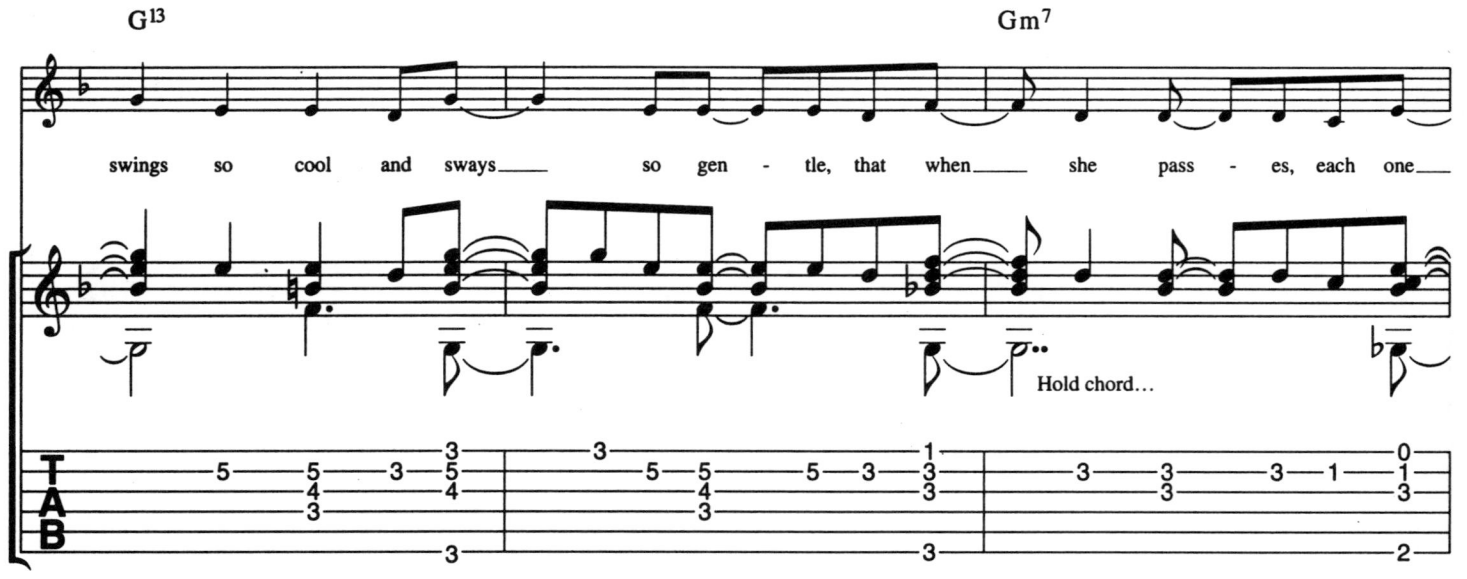
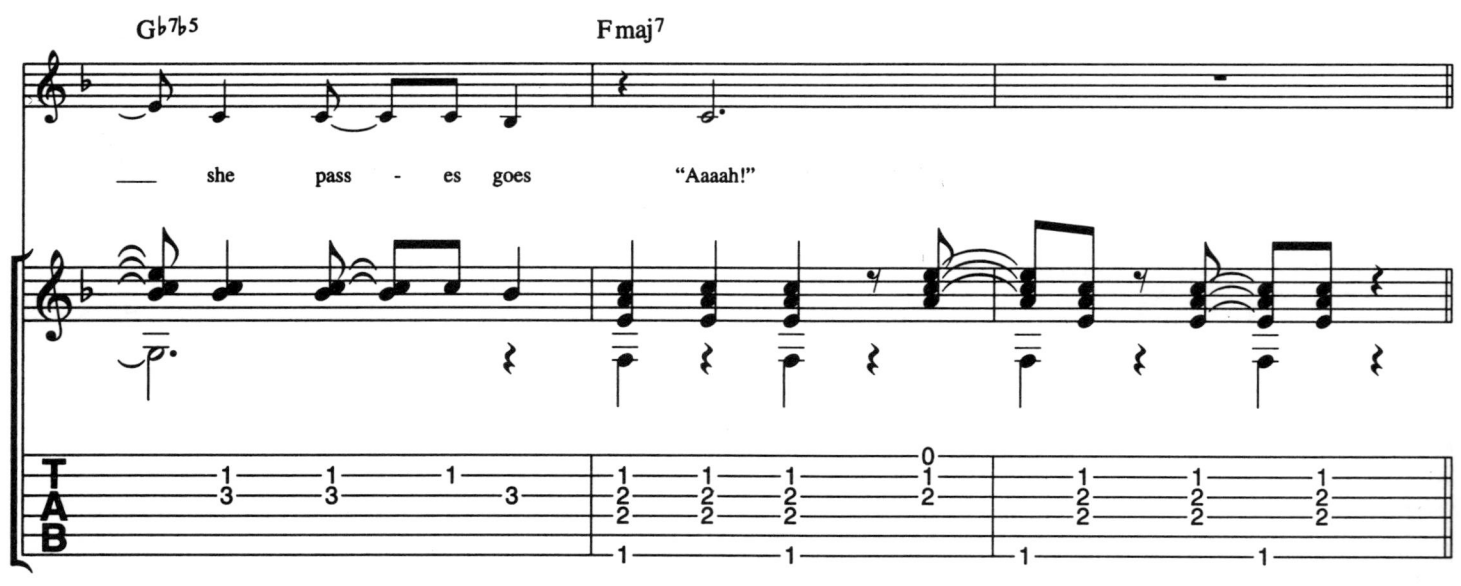
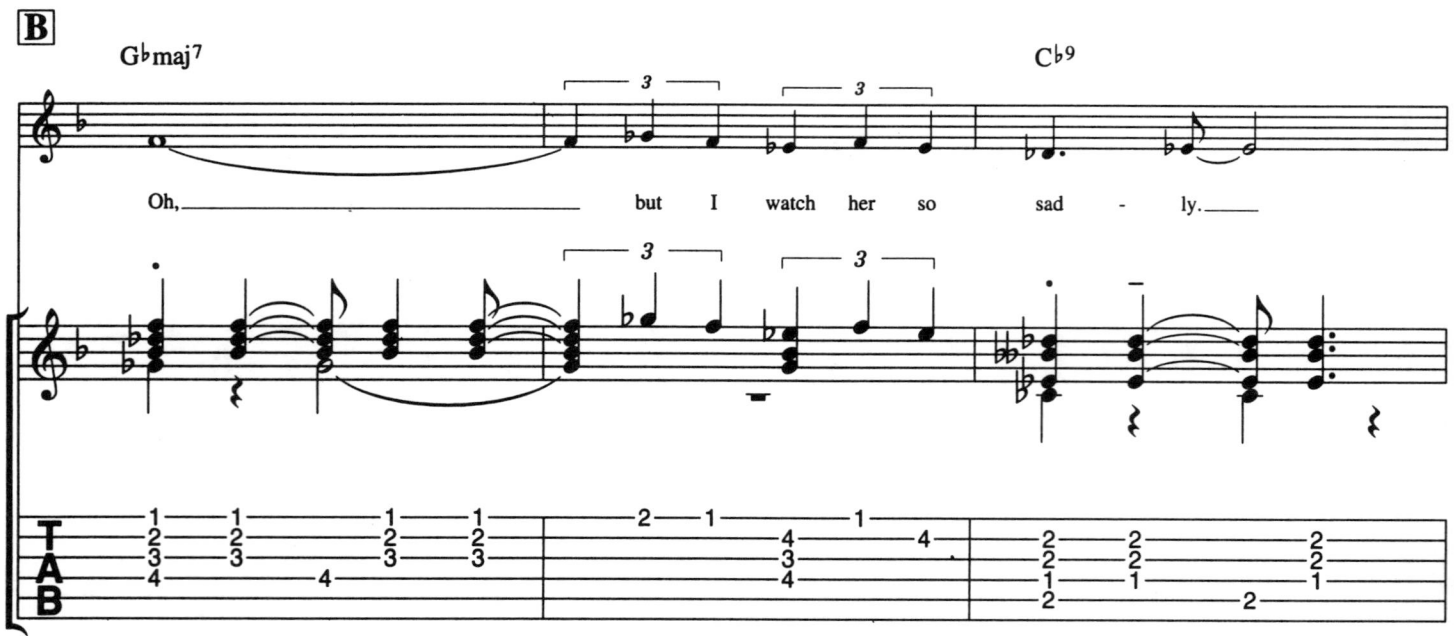

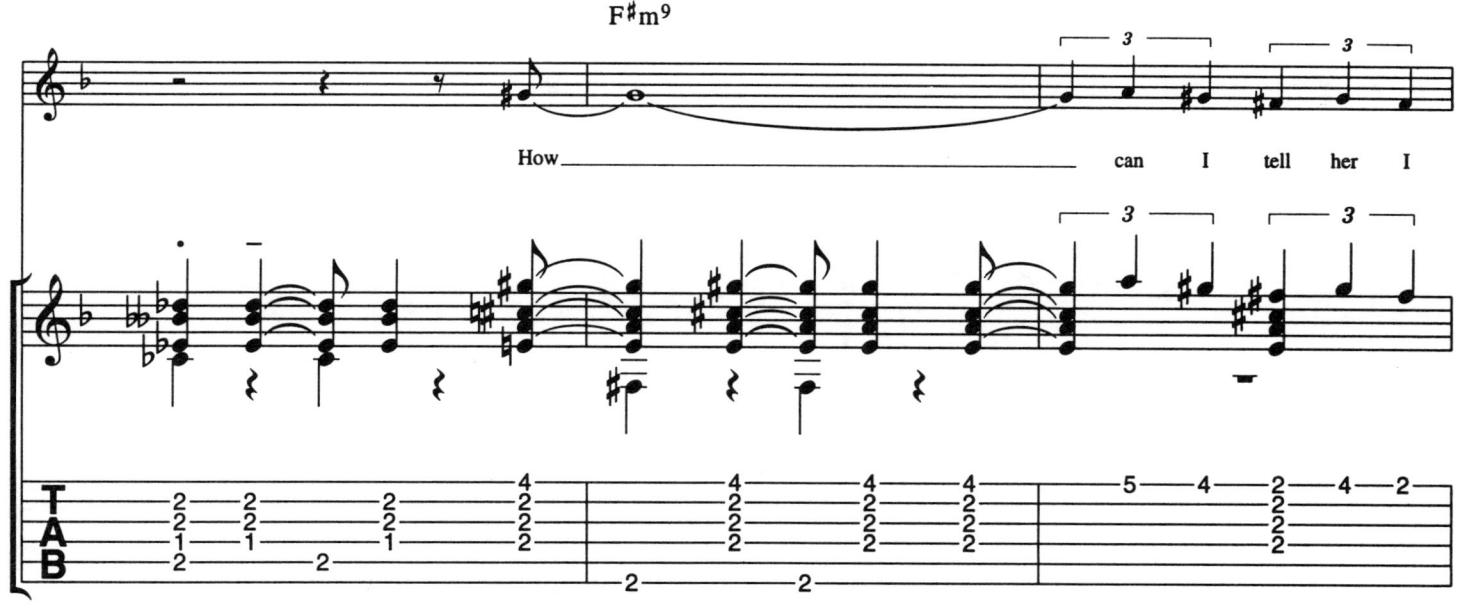
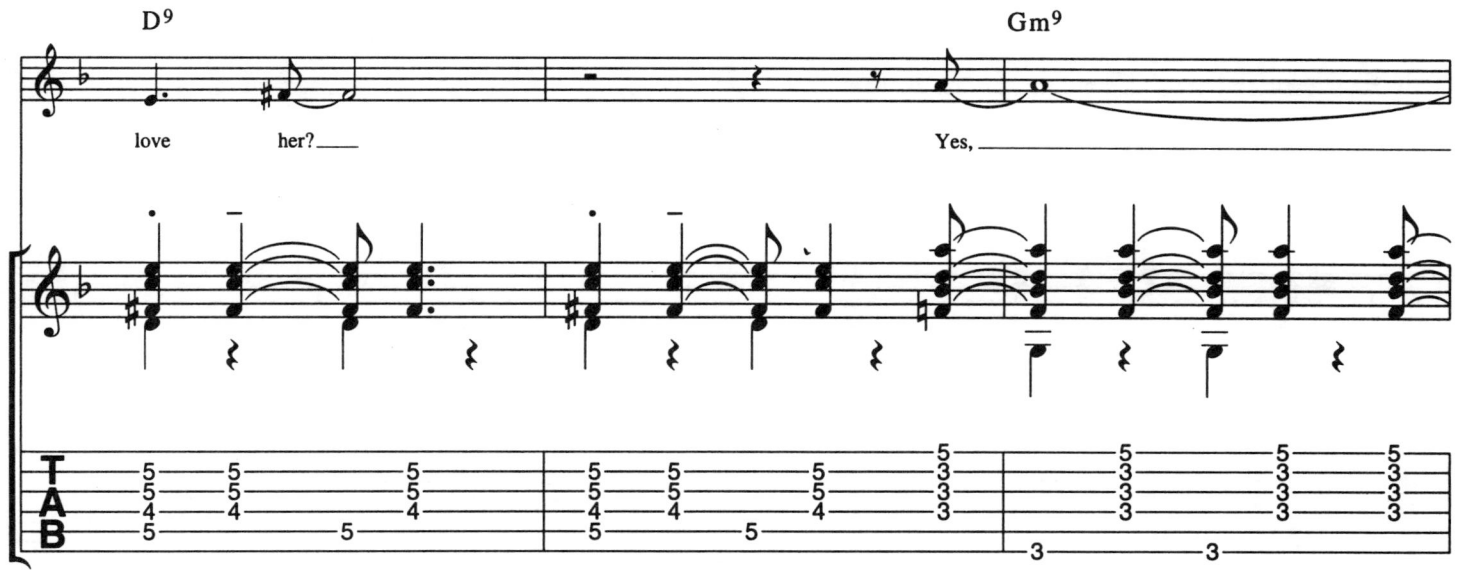

47

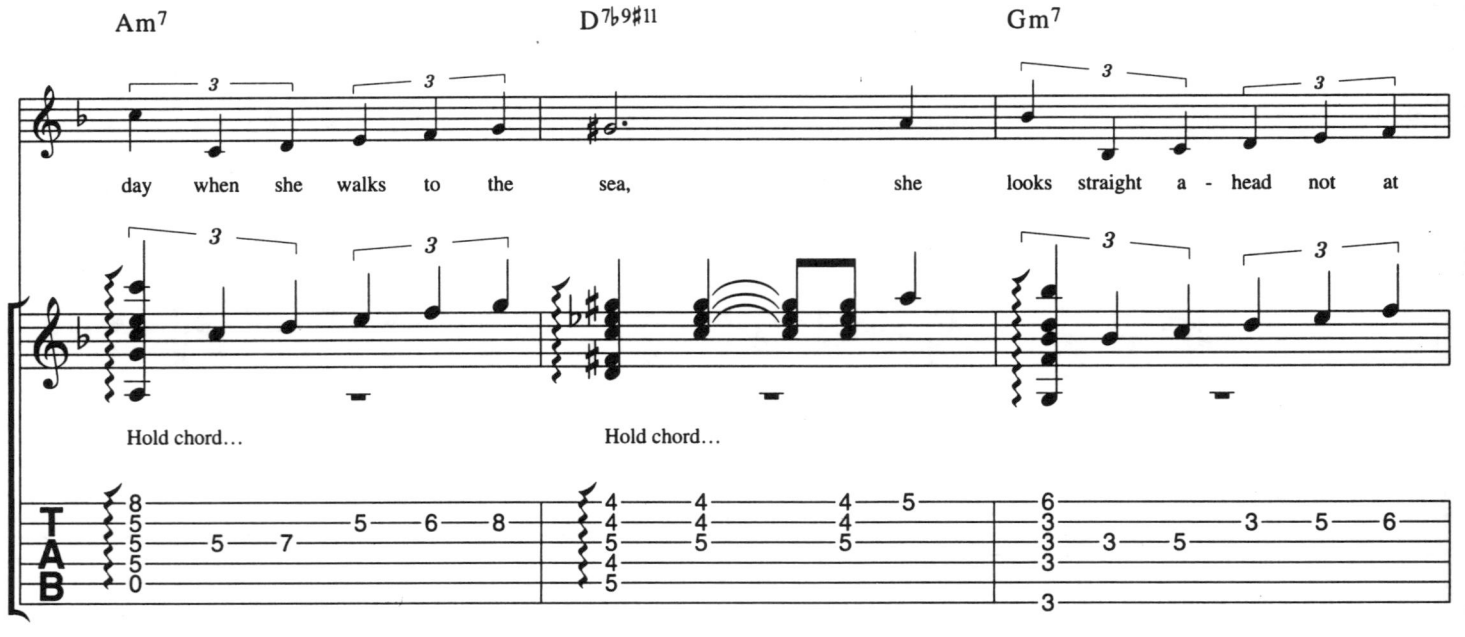
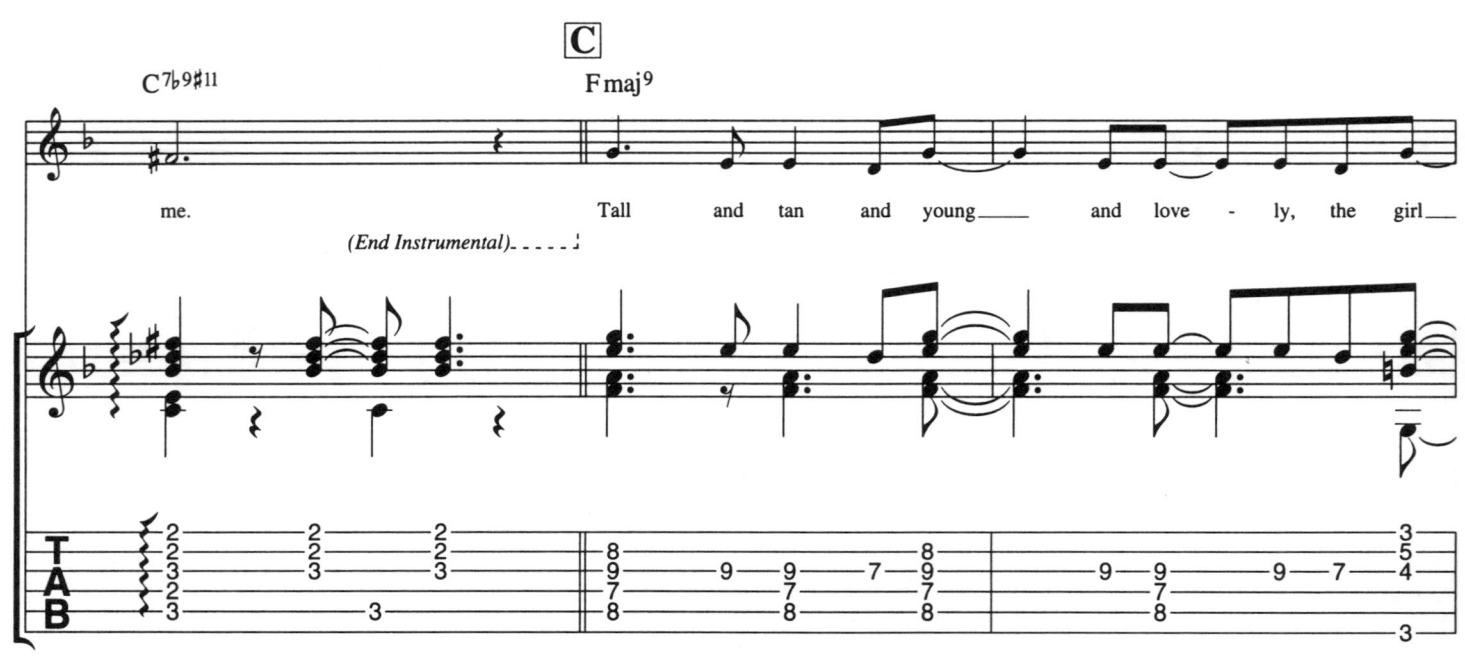

desafinado
(slightly out of tune)

english lyric by jon hendricks & jessie cavanaugh
music by antonio carlos jobim

Desfinado literally means 'off key'. This song is the anthem of the Bossa Nova (New Thing) beat and although to start with it was not accepted by the established musicians in Brazil, it became a massive international hit.

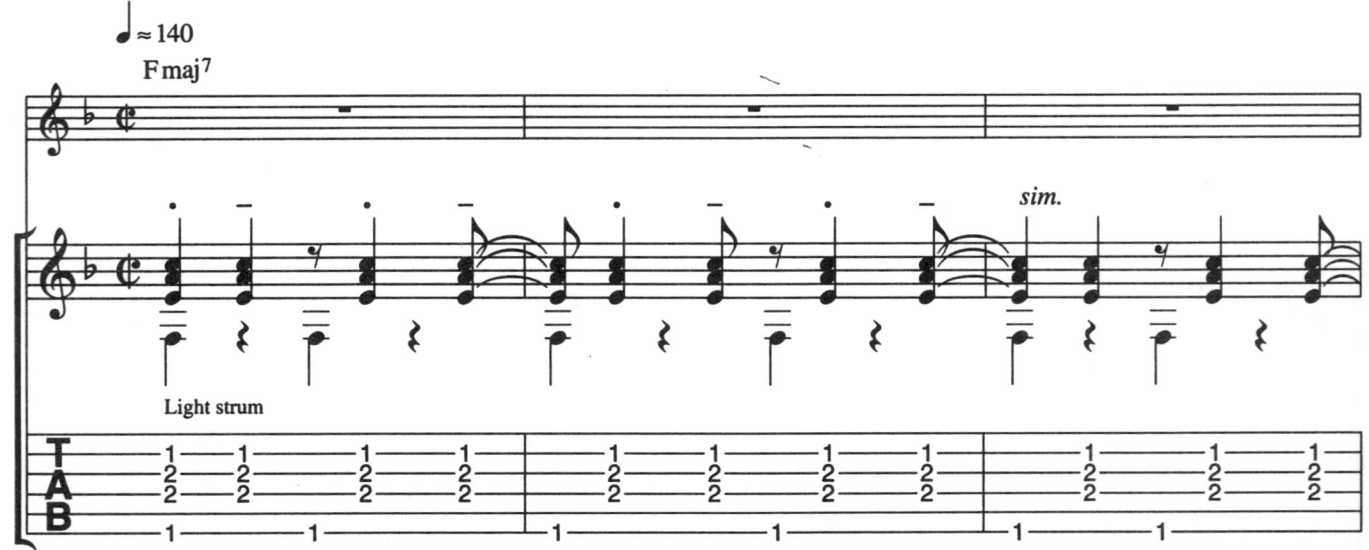

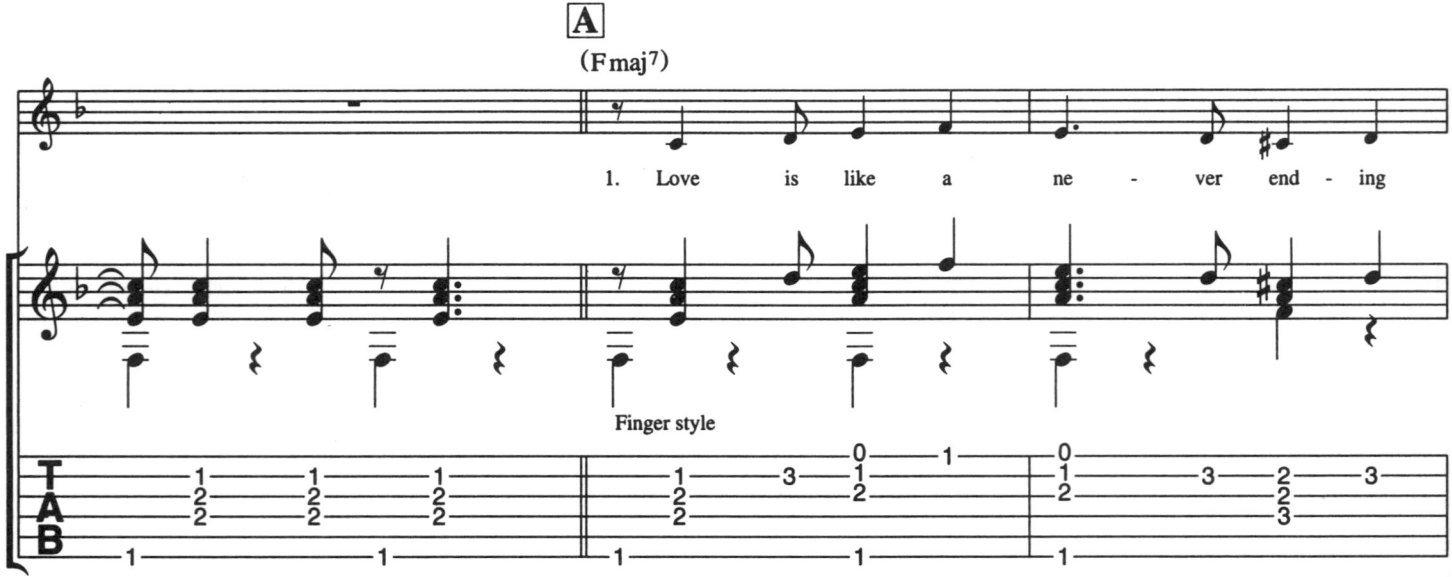

© copyright 1959 editora musical arapua, brazil
copyright 1962 with english lyric hollis music incorporated, usa
assigned to tro-essex music limited, suite 2.07, plaza 535 kings road, london sw10 for the british commonwealth
(excluding canada and australasia) also the republics of ireland and south africa
all rights reserved
international copyright secured

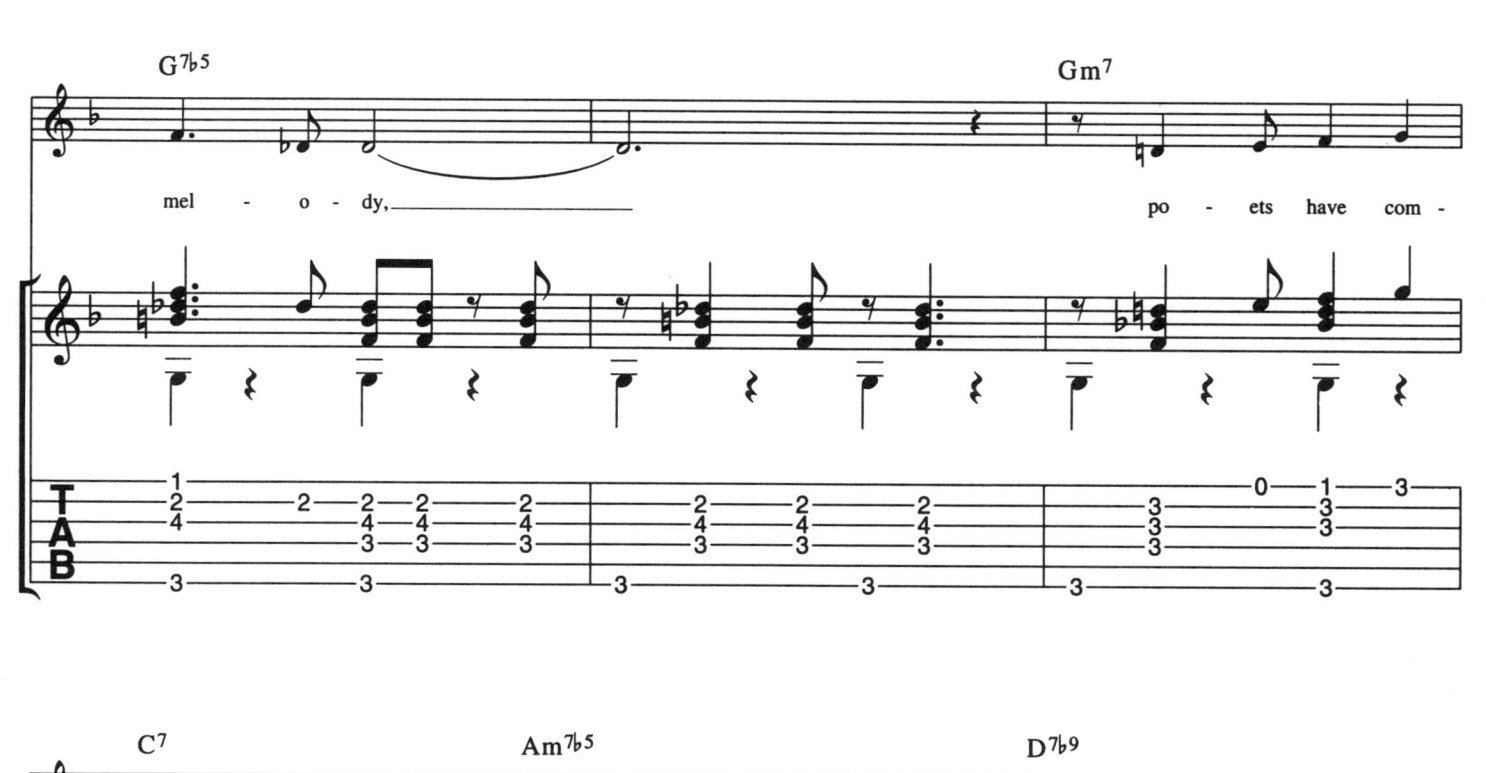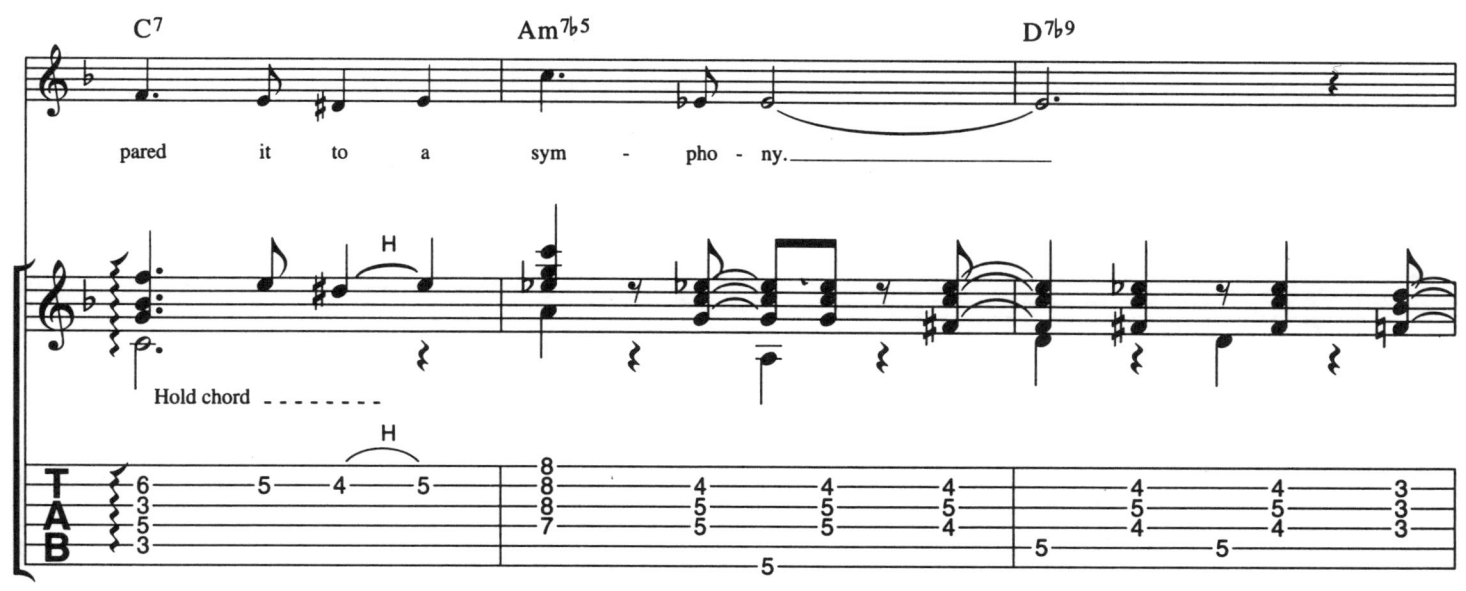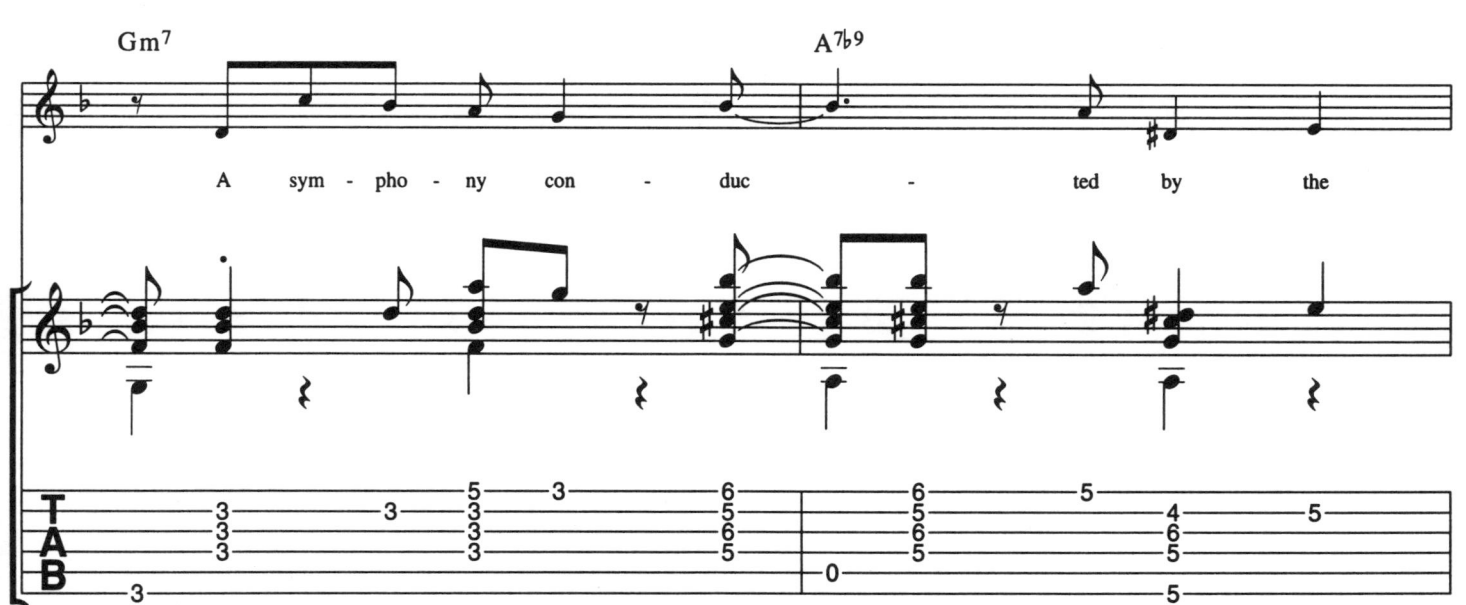

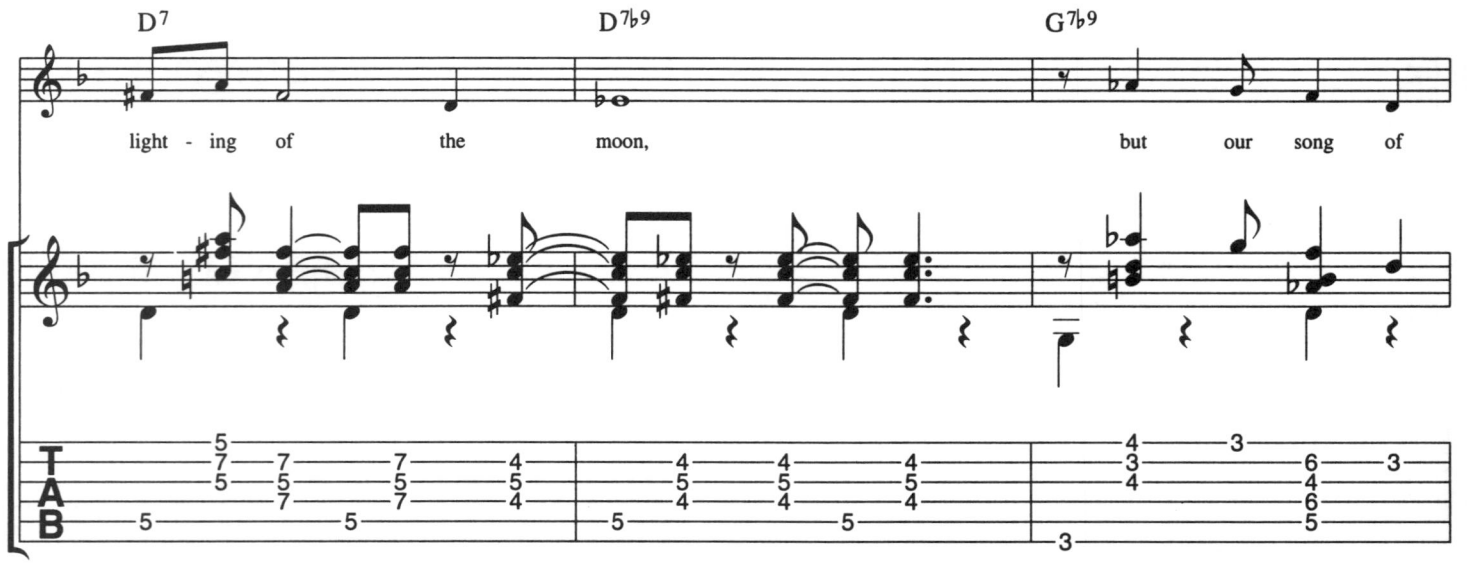

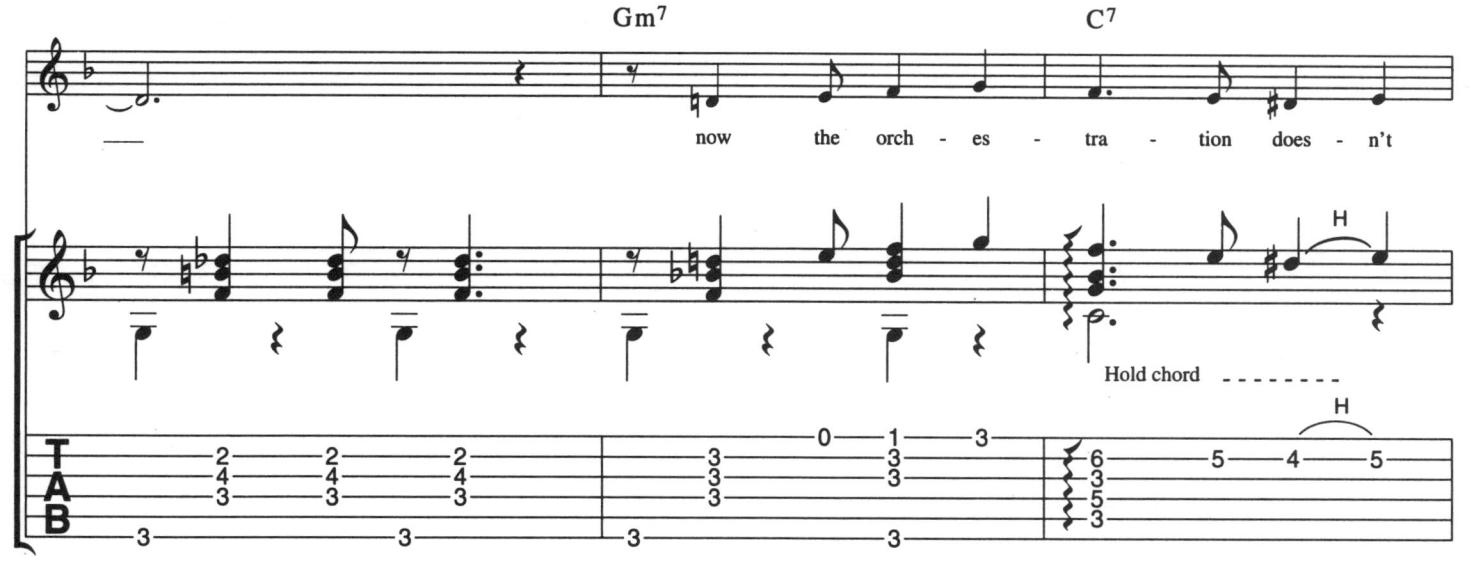
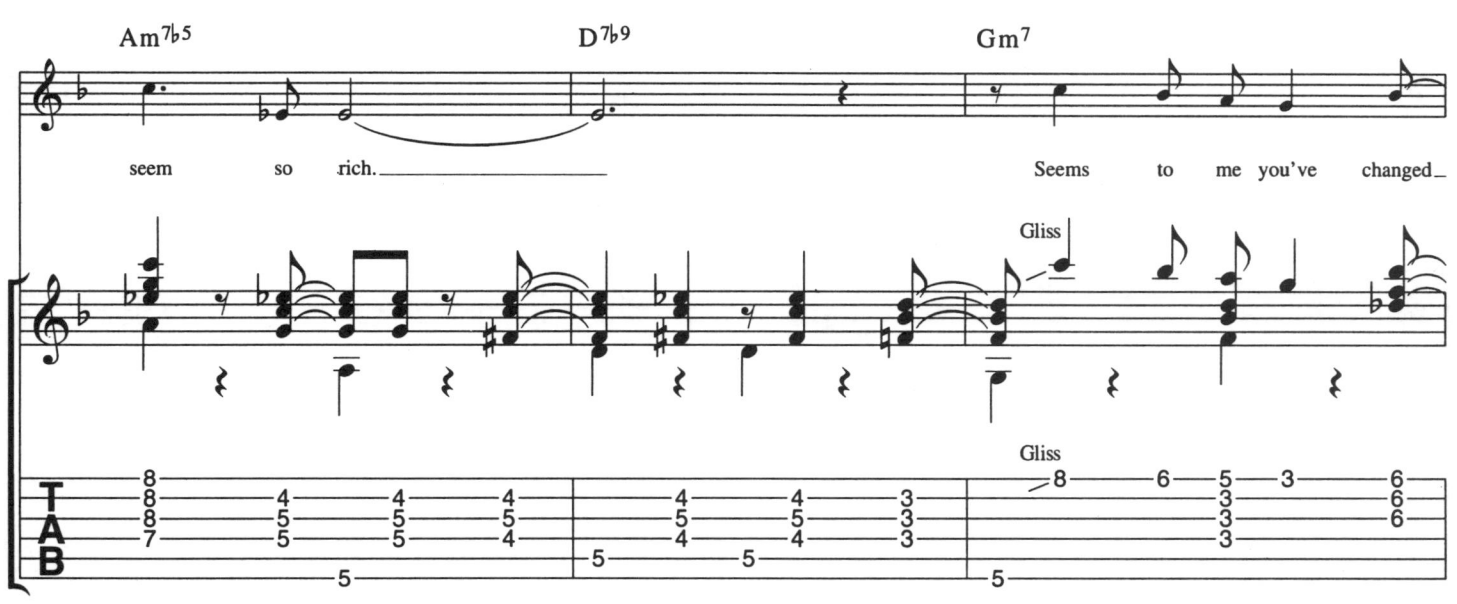
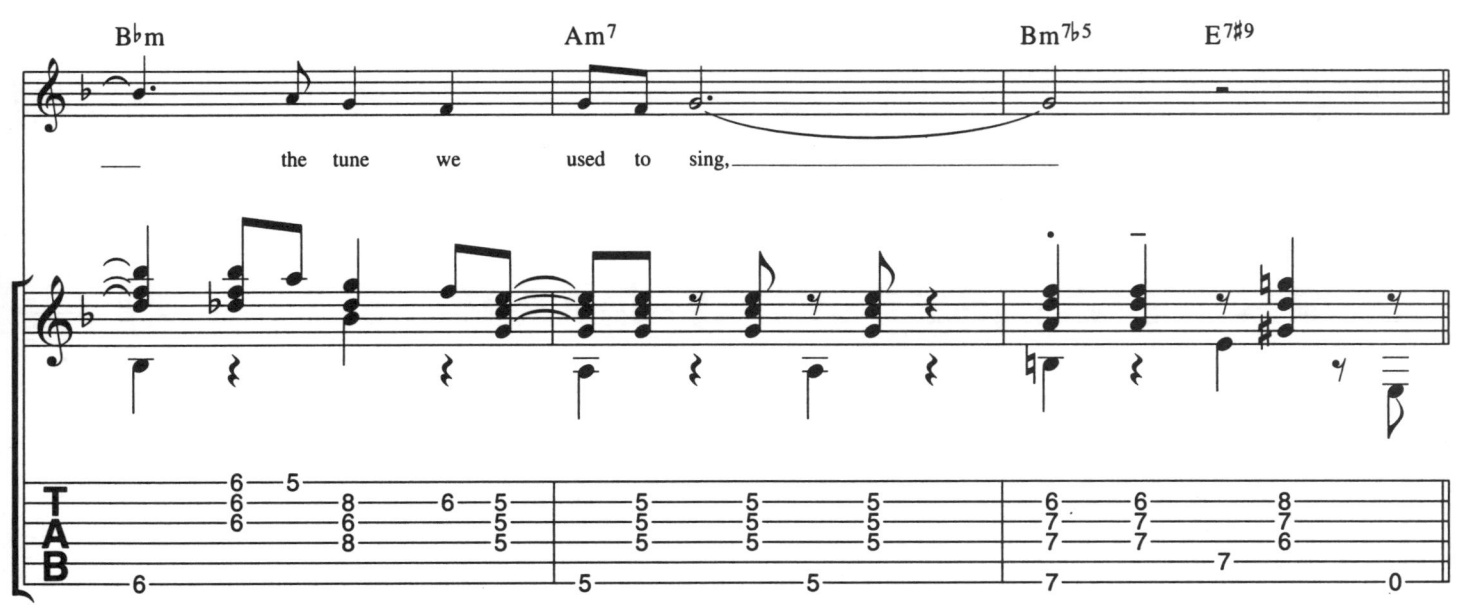

53

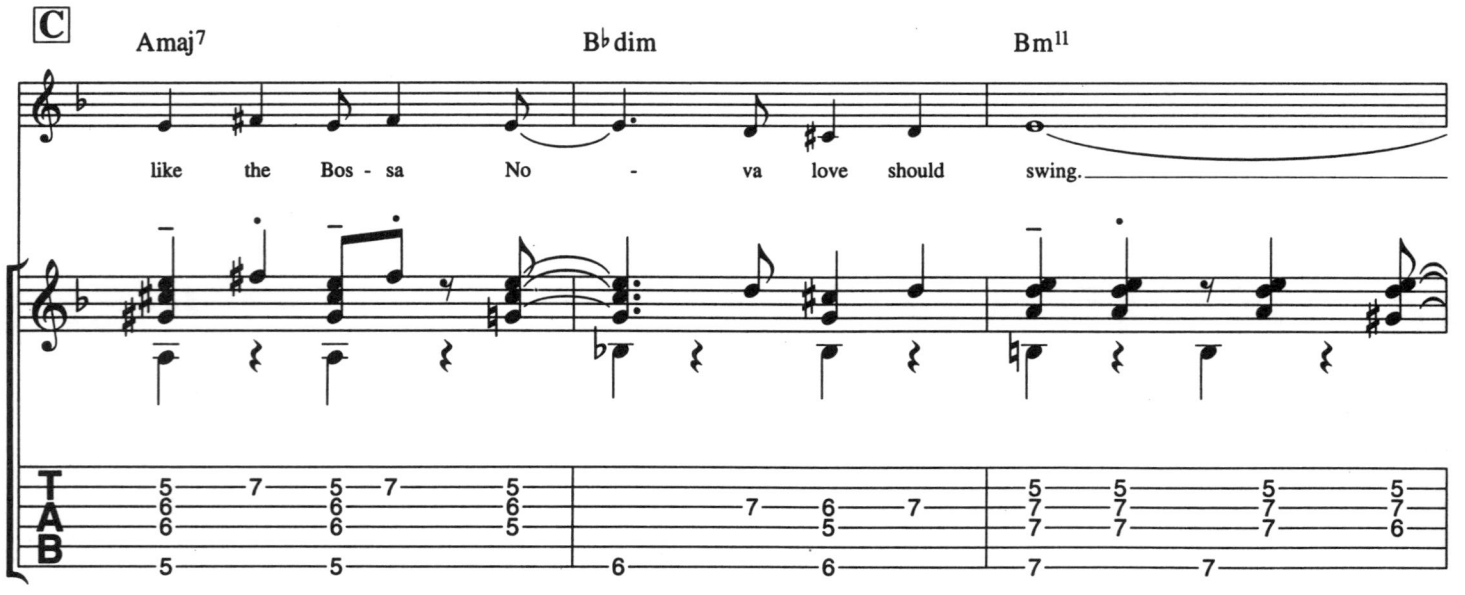

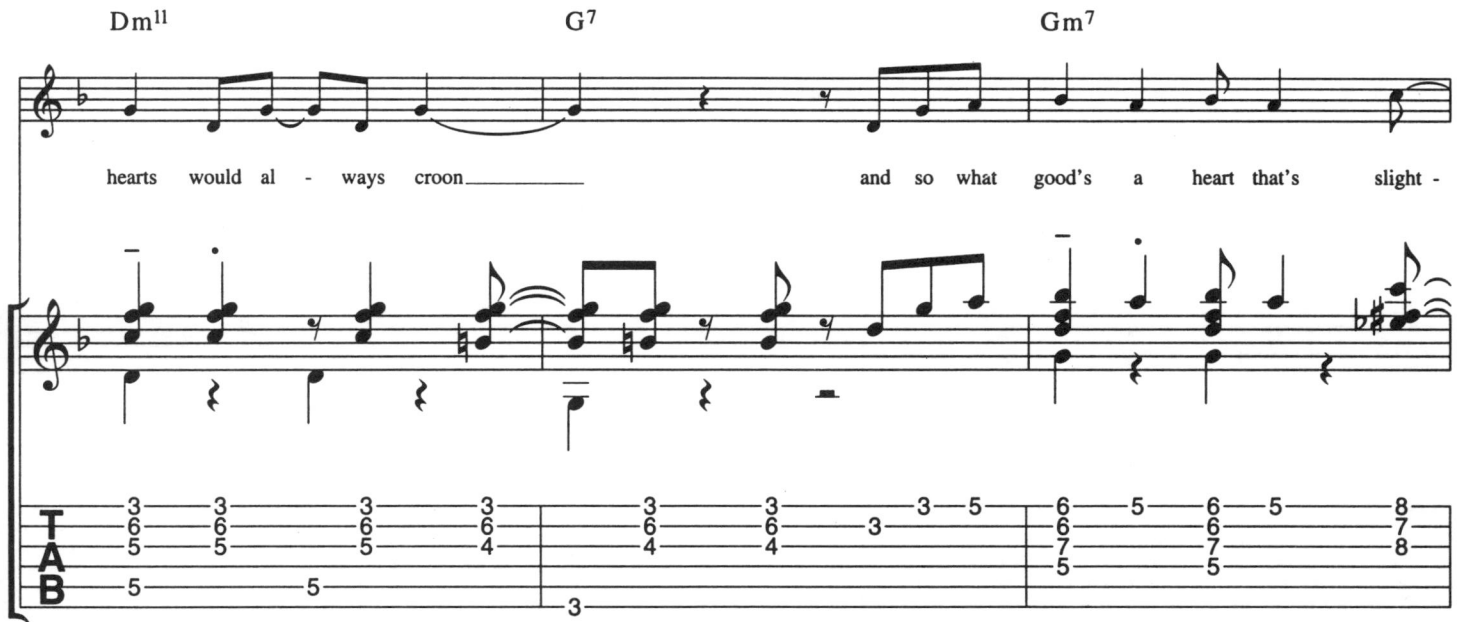

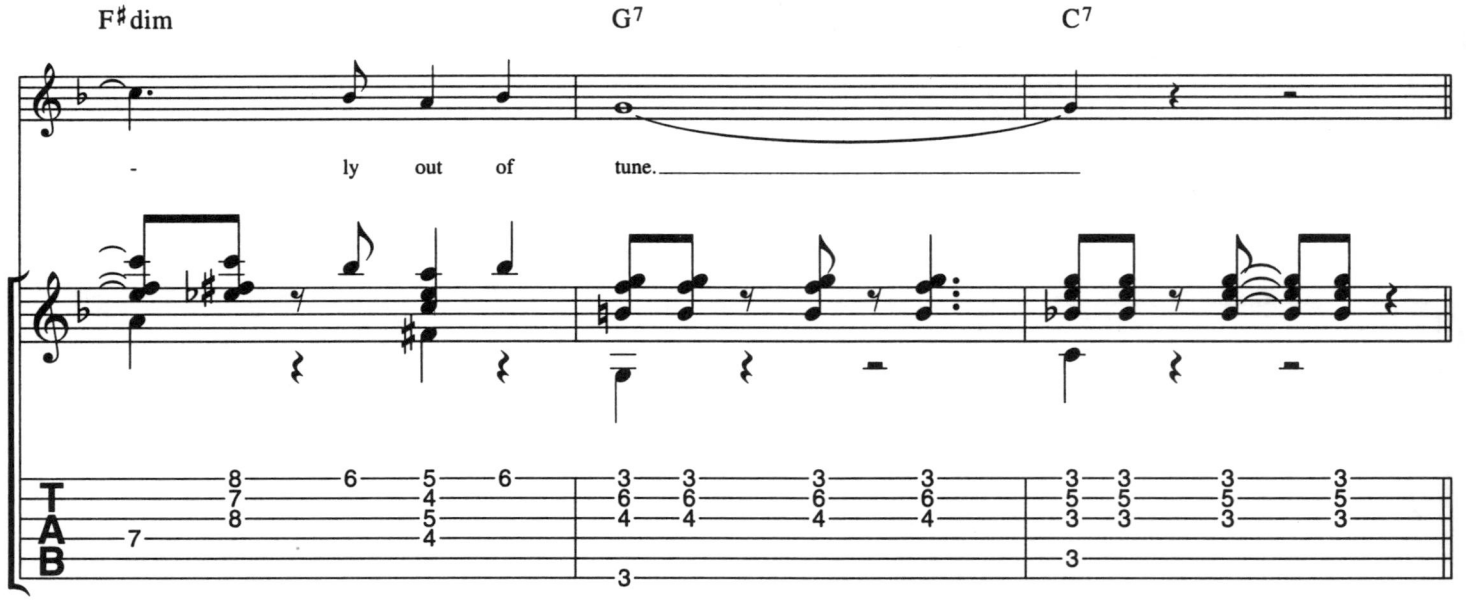
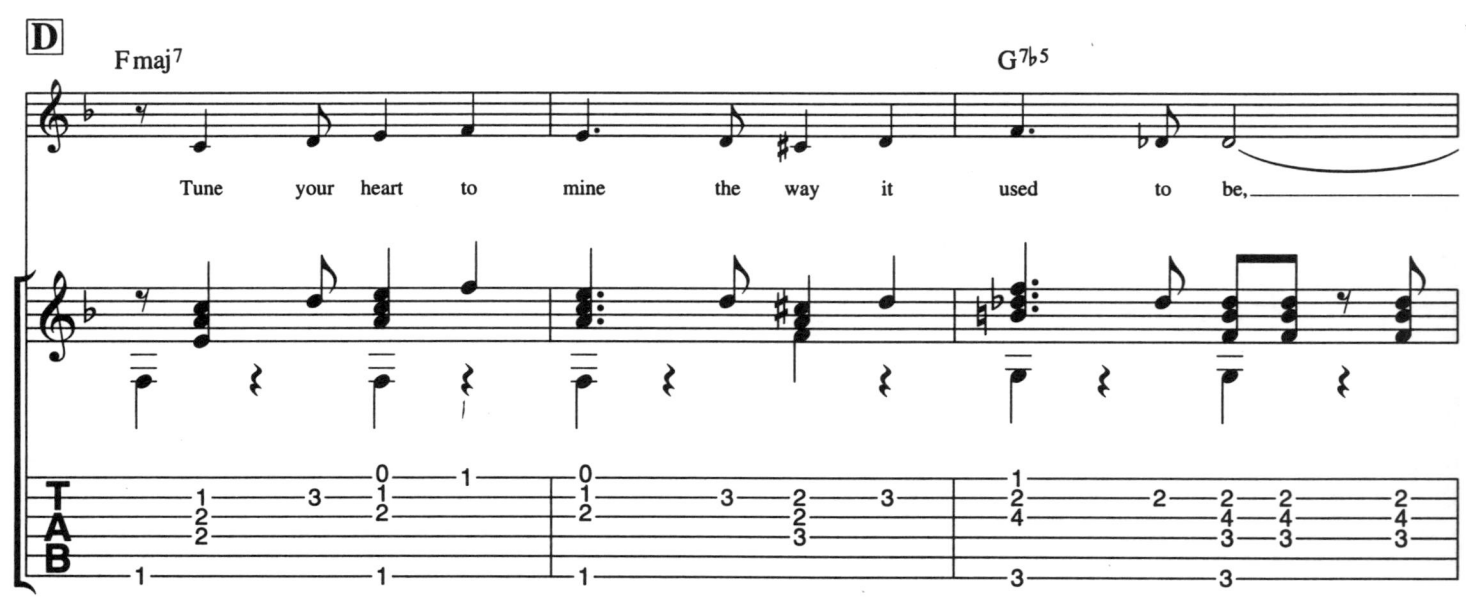

56

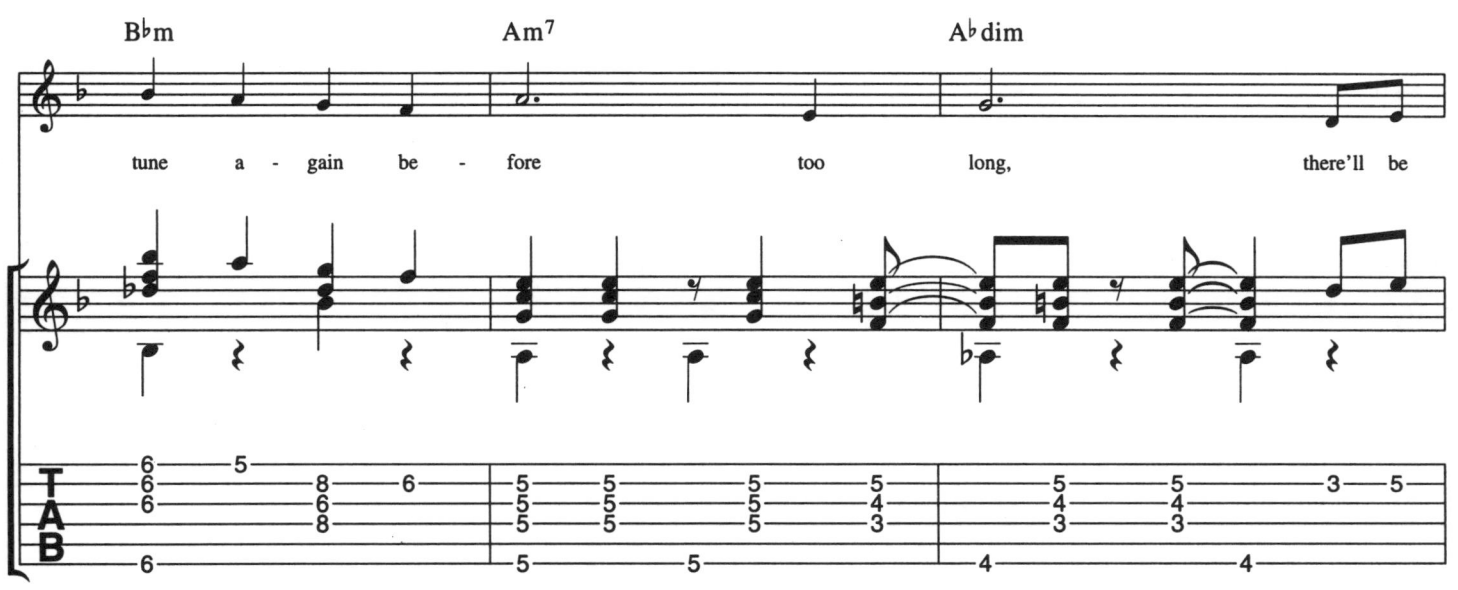
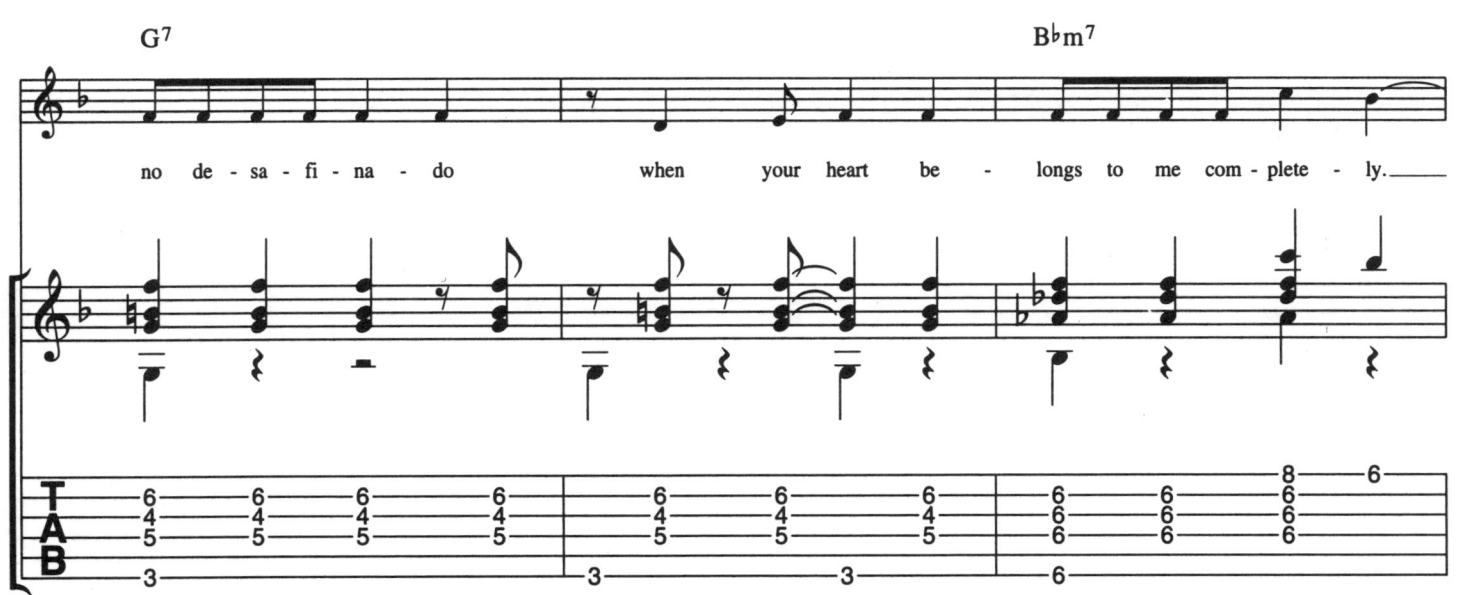

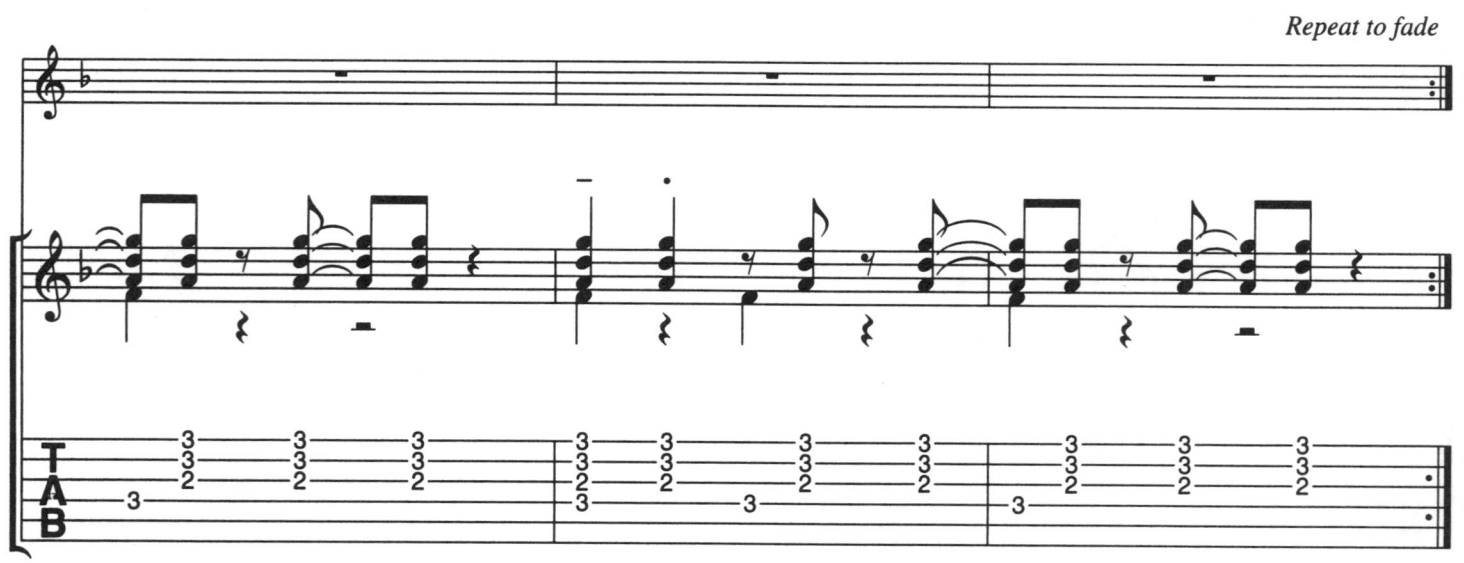

water to drink (agua de beber)

words by norman gimbel
music by antonio carlos jobim

This arrangement keeps the basis of Jobim's original accompaniment and adds melody. The rhythm should be percussive and a certain amount of freedom should be exercised to give the song feeling.

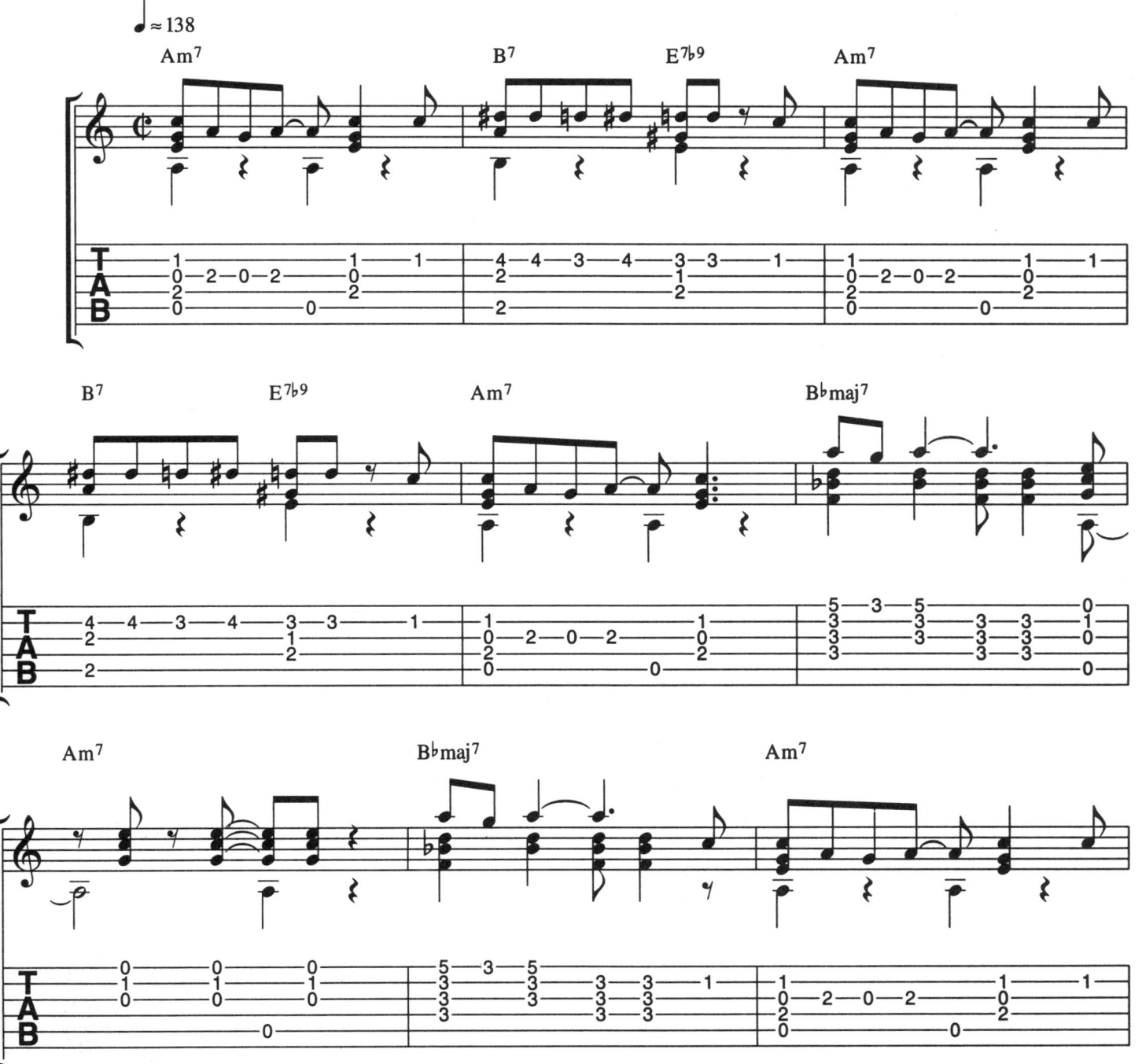

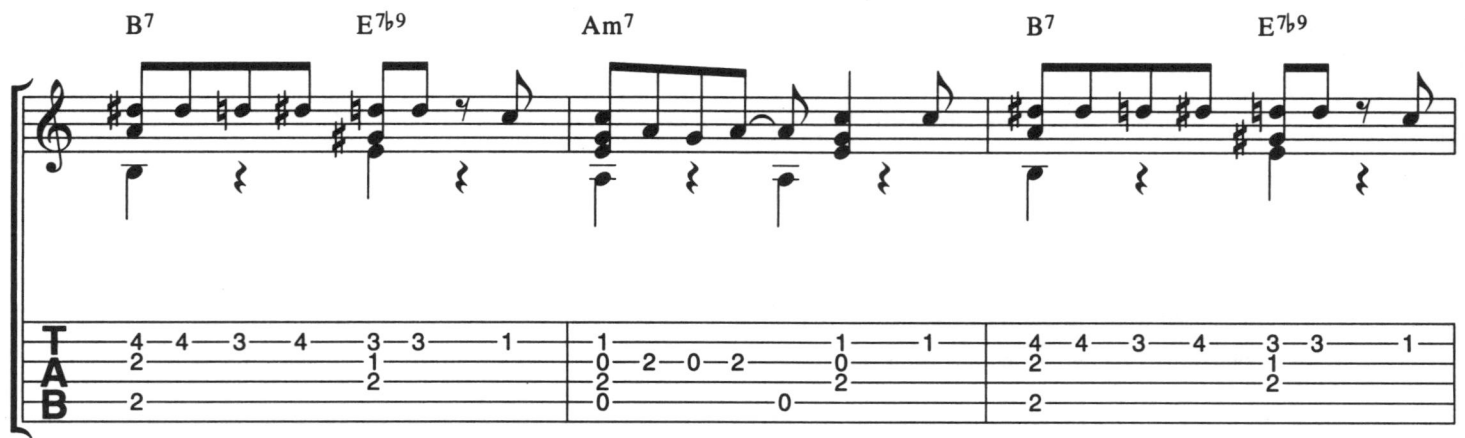
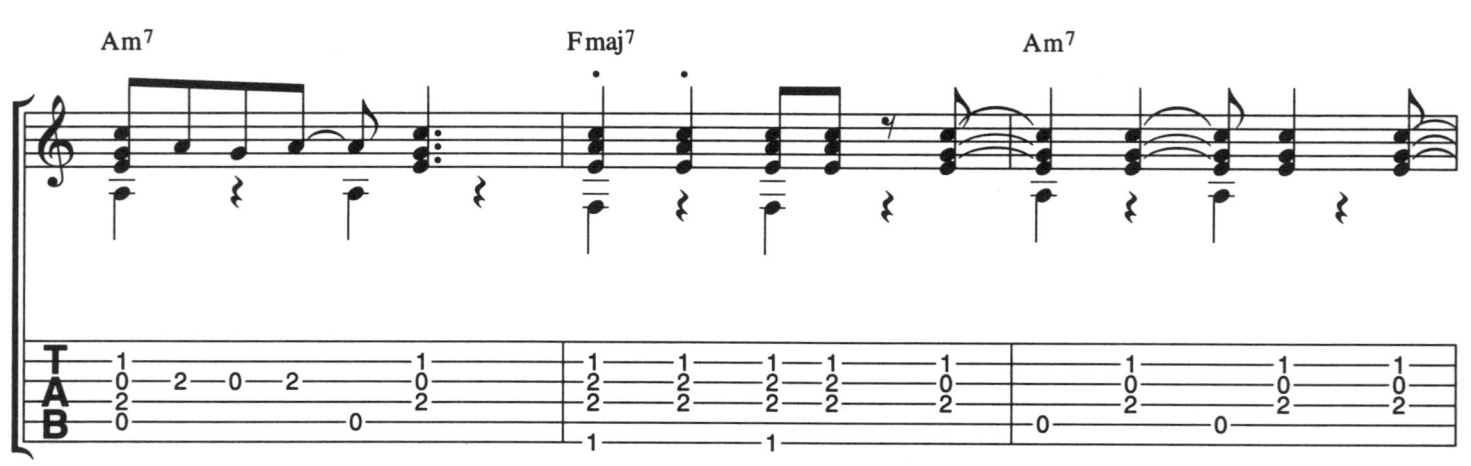
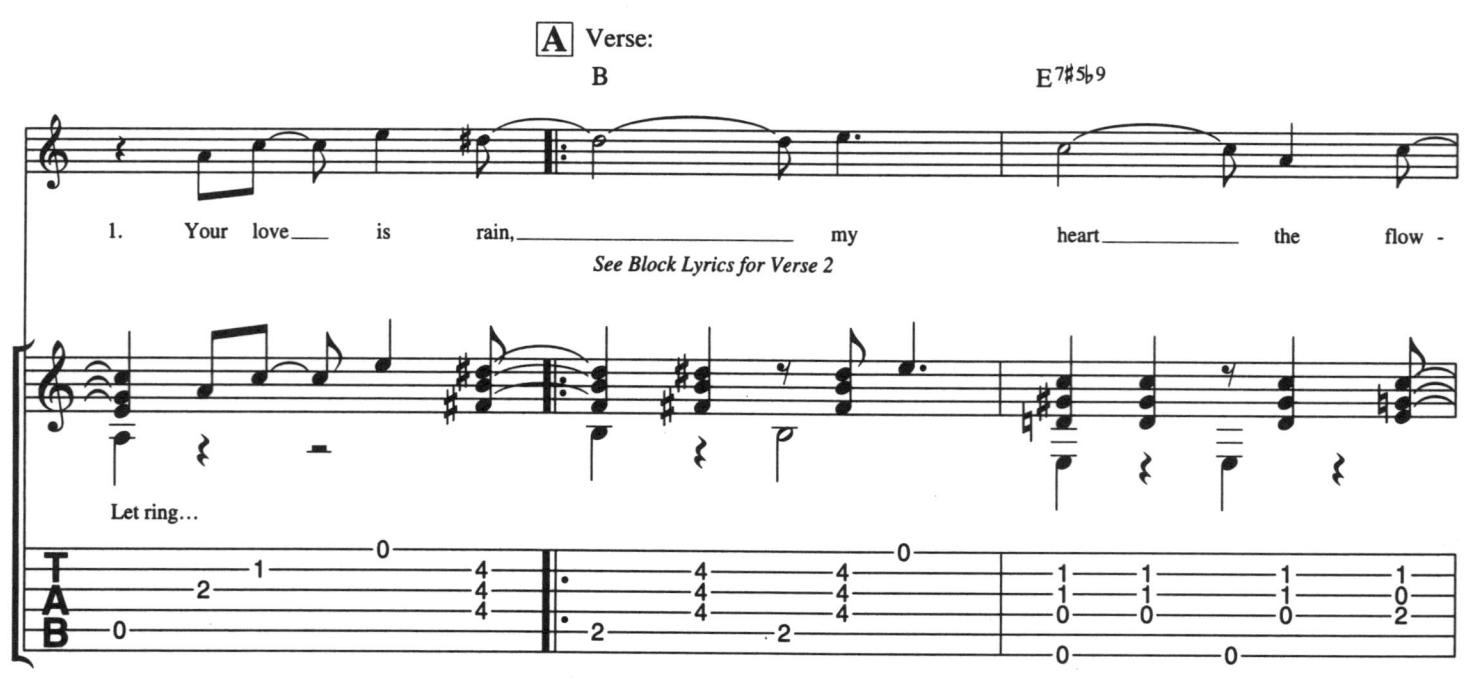

A Verse:

1. Your love is rain, my heart the flow-

See Block Lyrics for Verse 2

Let ring...

60

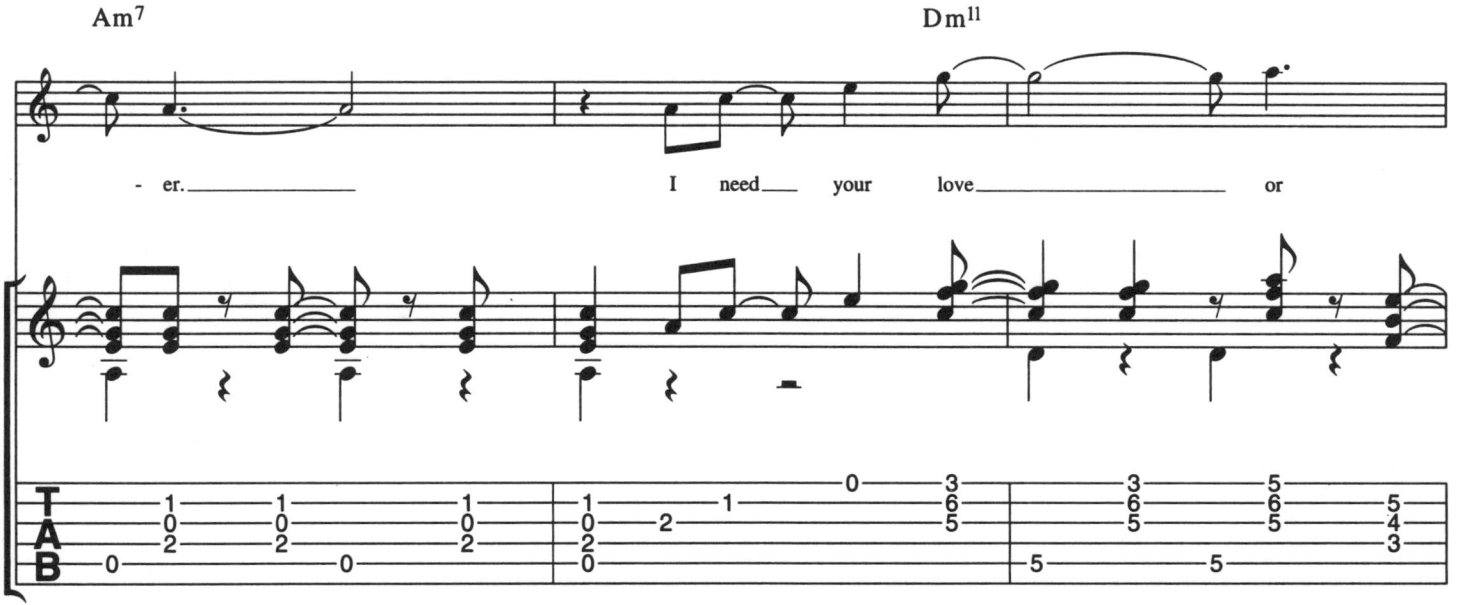
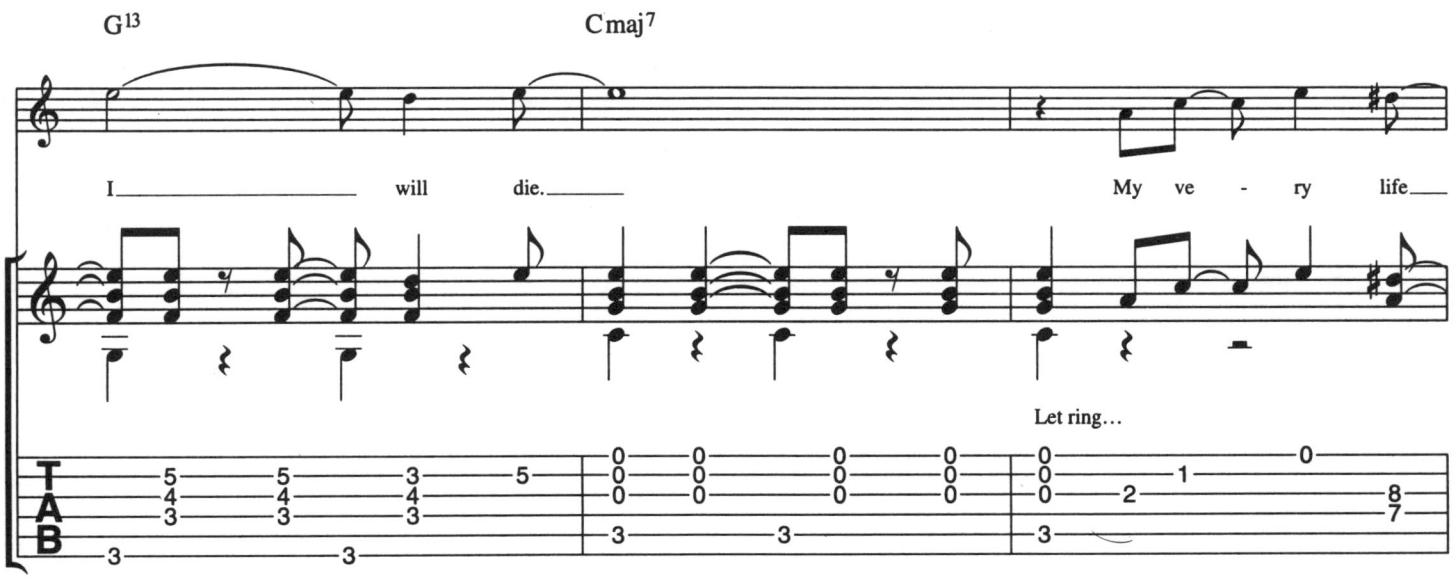
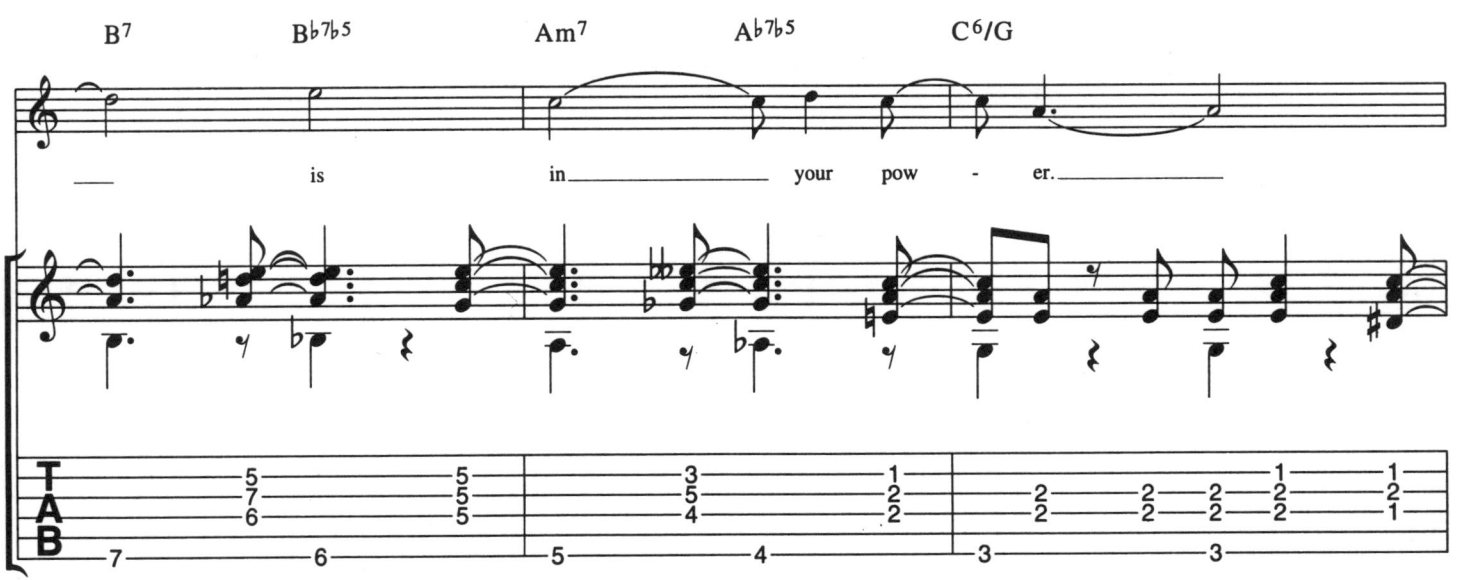

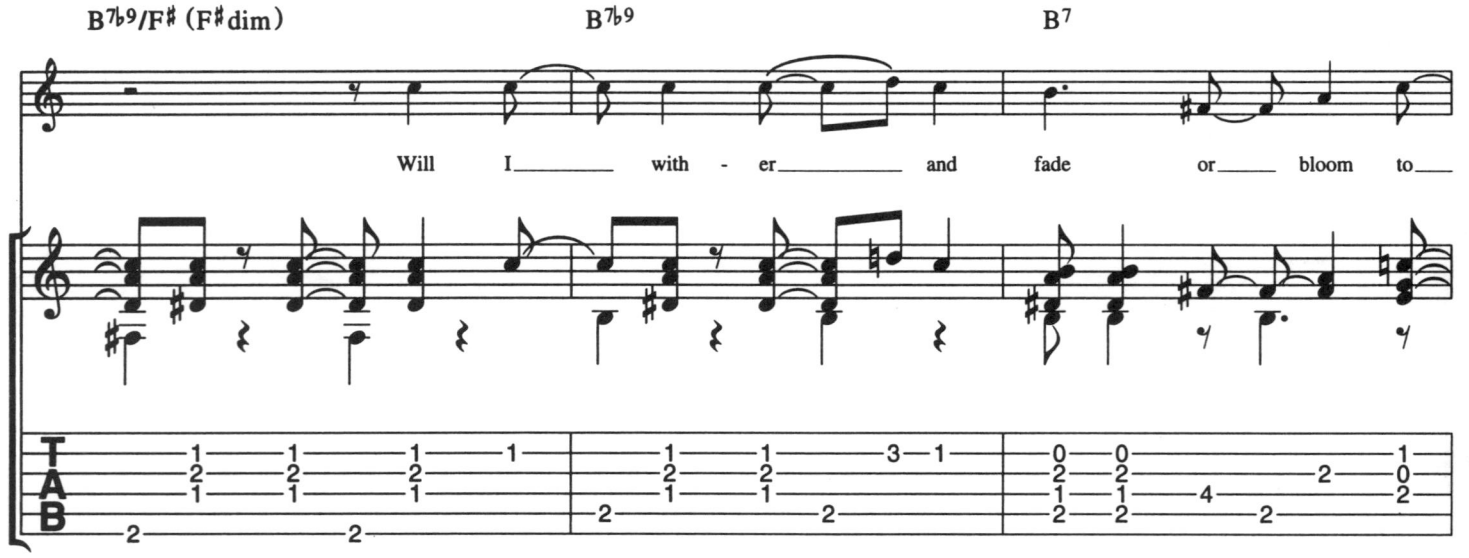
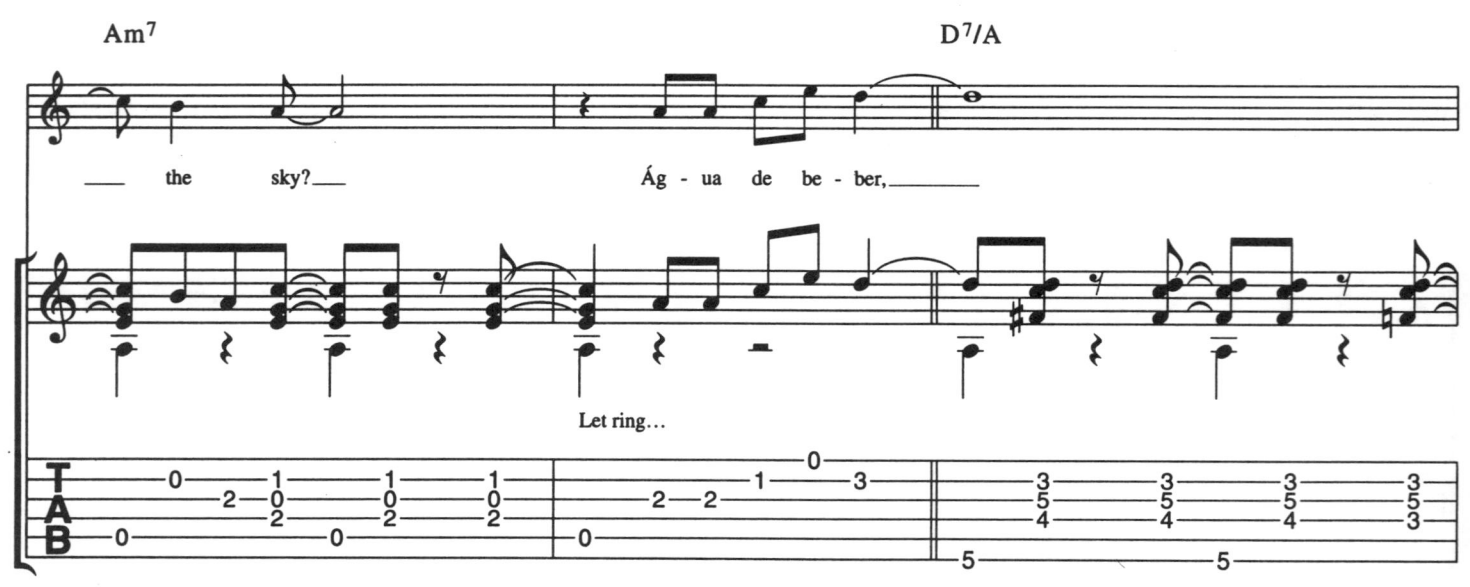
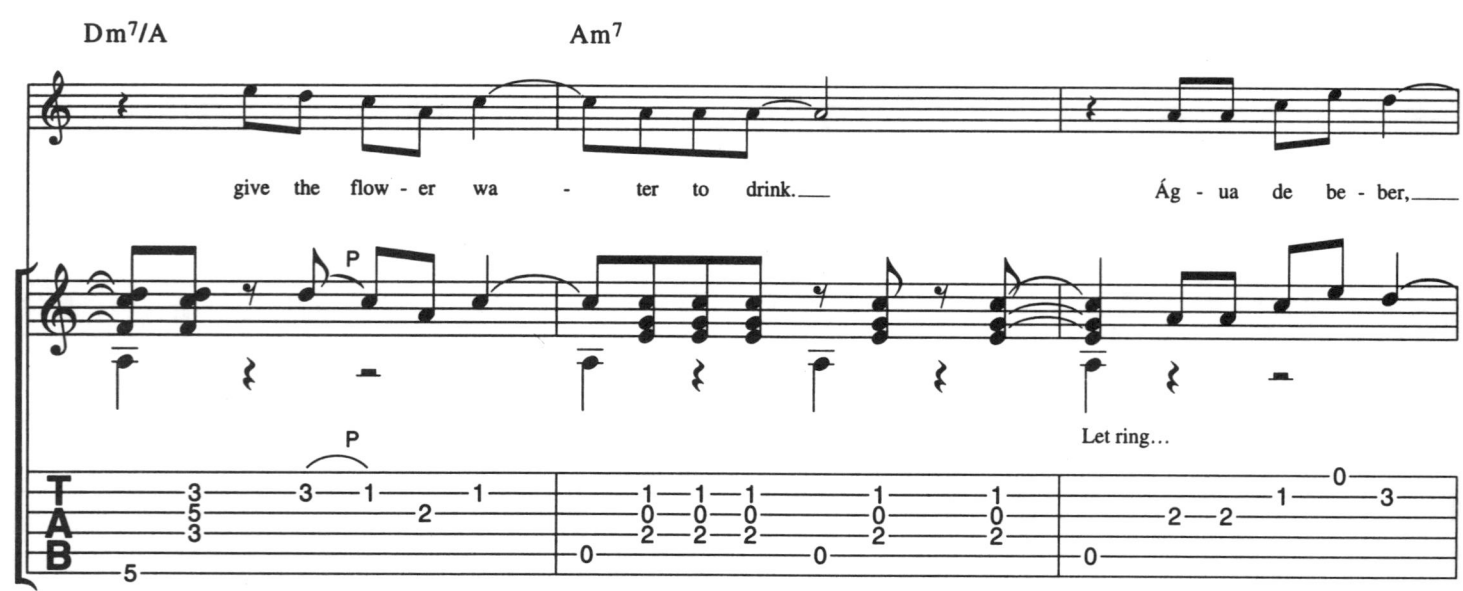

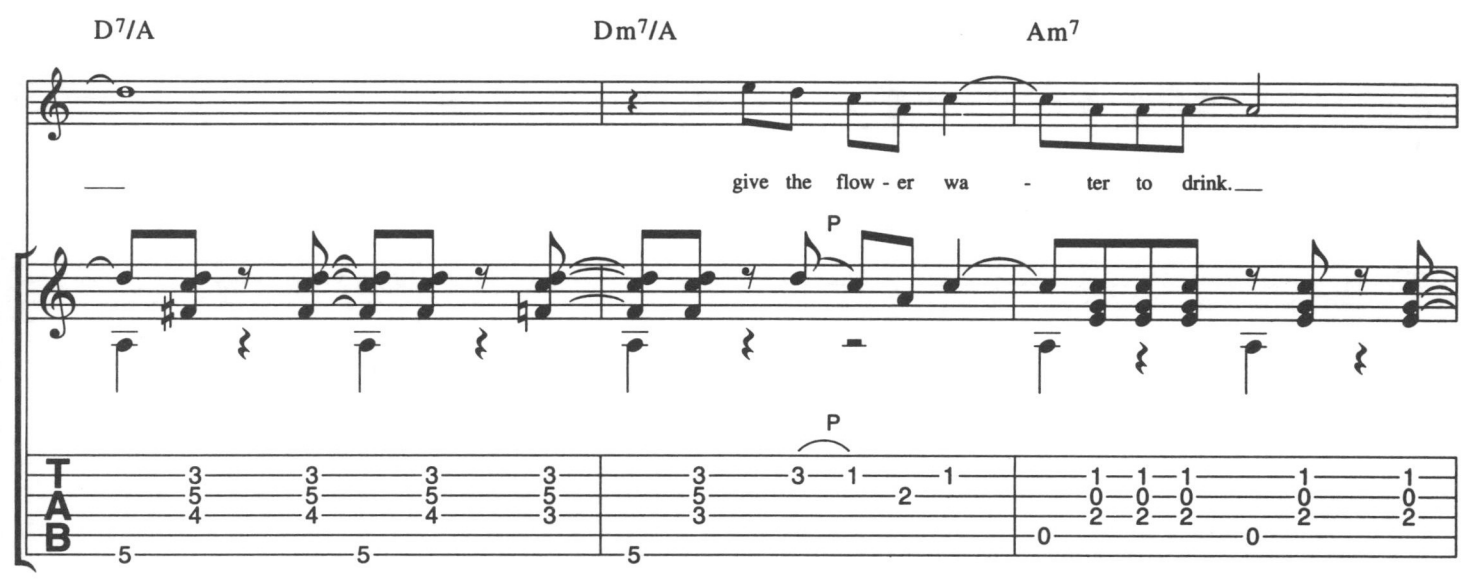
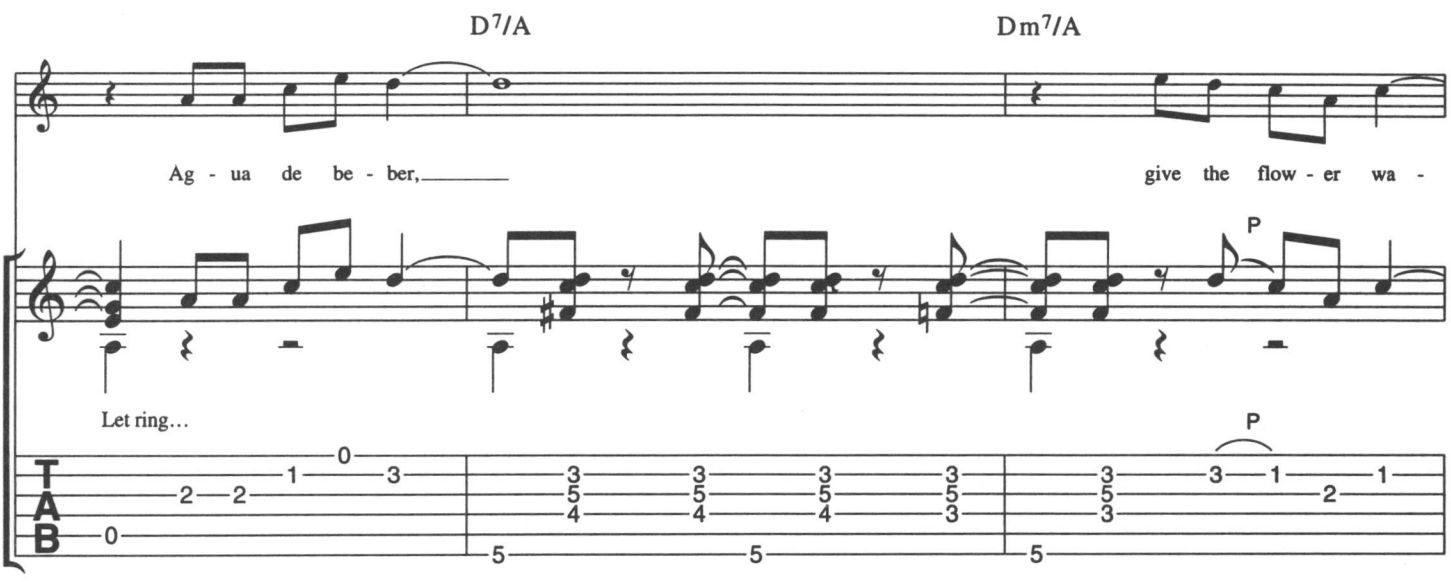

63

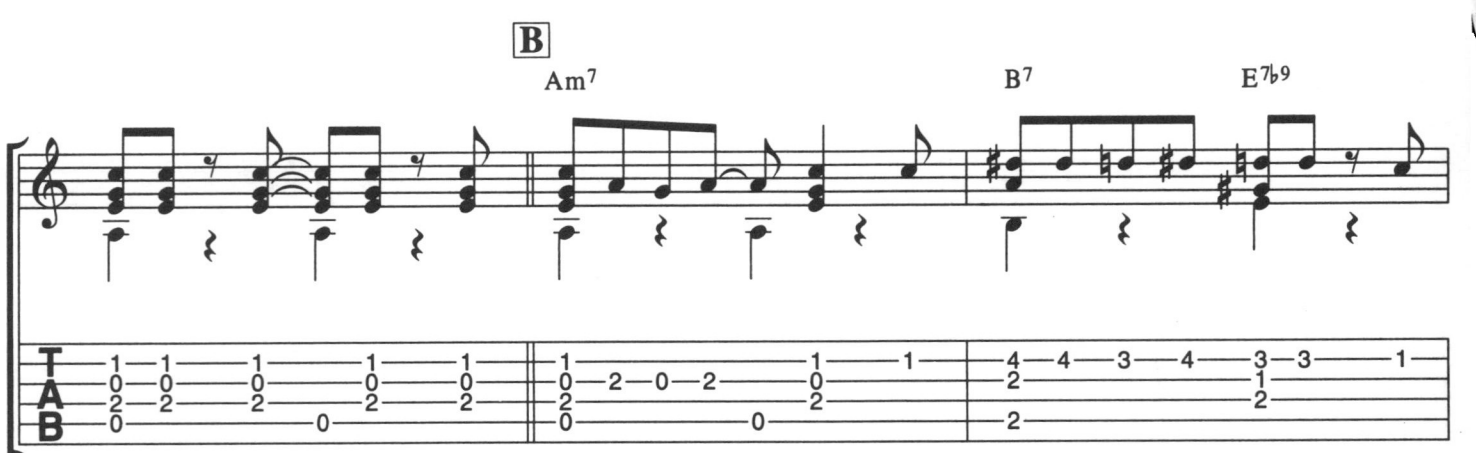
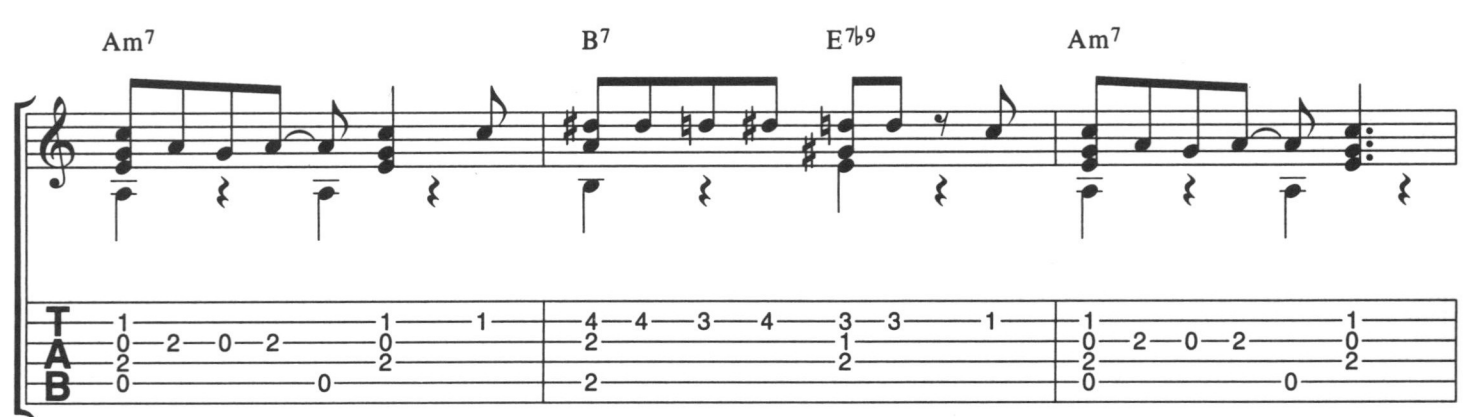
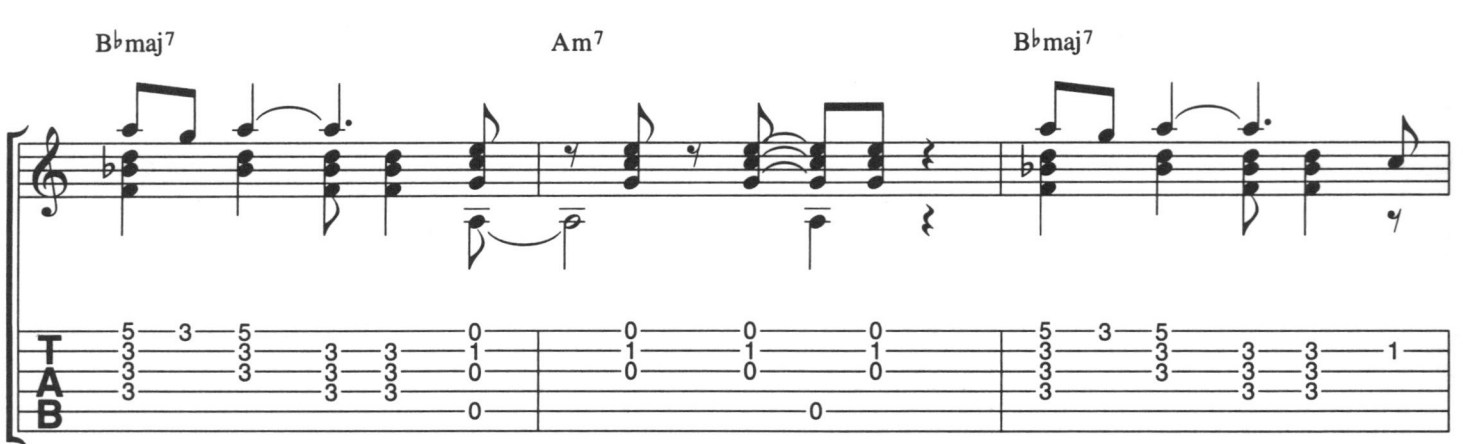
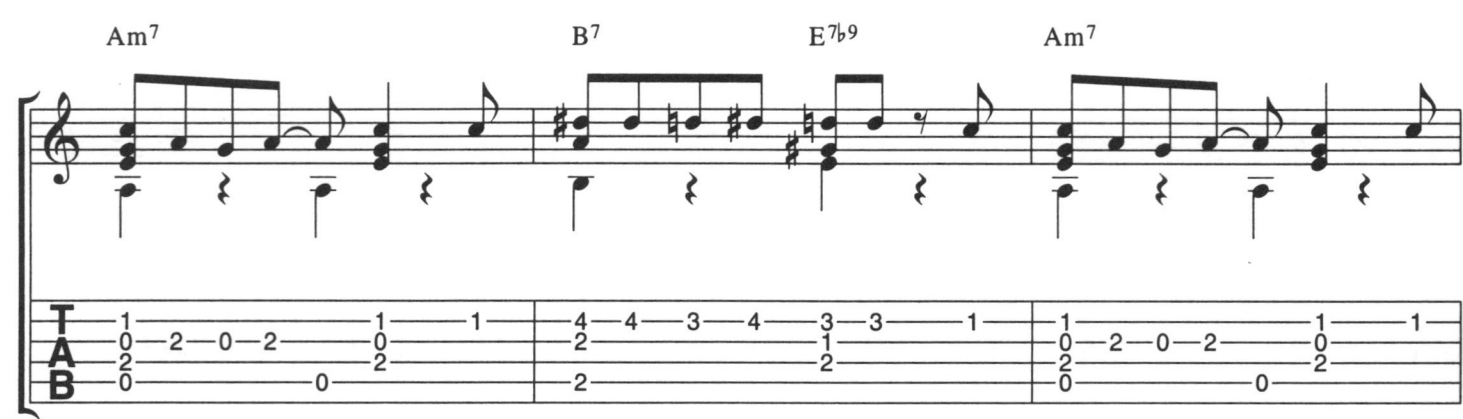

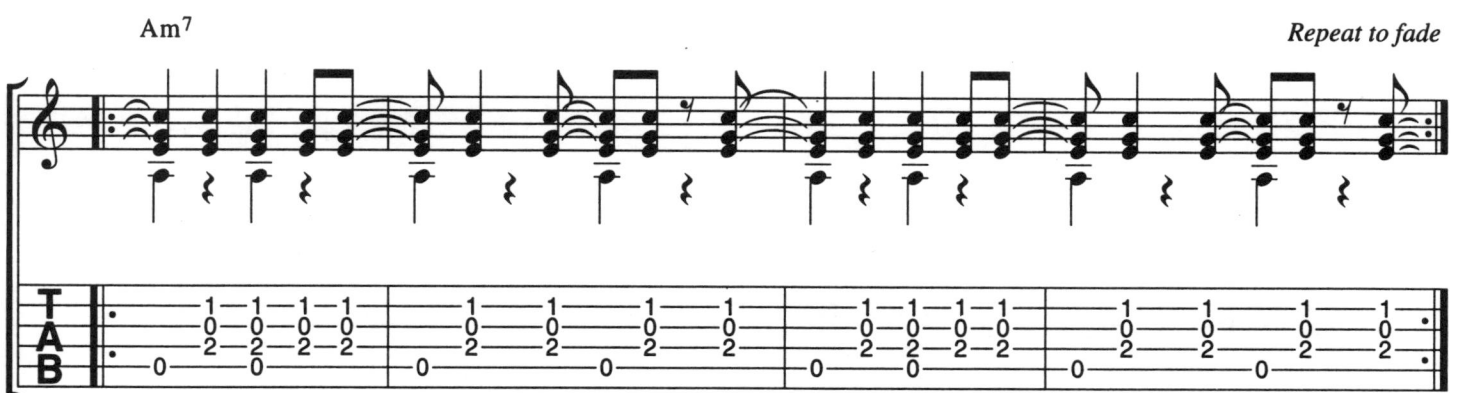

Verse 2:
The rain can fall on distant deserts
The rain can fall upon the sea
The rain can fall upon the flower
Since the rain has to fall let it fall on me.

Água de beber
Água de beber camará
Água de beber
Água de beber camará
Água de beber
Água de beber camará.

Portuguese lyrics

Eu quis amar Mas tive medo
E quis salvar meu corração
Mas o amor sabe um segredo
O medo pode matar o seu coração

Água de beber...

Eu nunca fiz coisa tão certa
Entrei pra escola do perdão
A minha casa vive aberta
Abre todas as portas do coração

Água de beber...

Eu sempre tive uma certeza
Que só me deu desilusão
É que o amor É uma tristeza
Muita mágoa demais para um coração

Água de beber...

wave (vou te contar)

words & music by antonio carlos jobim

A classic Jobim song that has become a jazz standard. It was originally recorded on the 1967 album of the same name. The opening rhythm sounds good if it is lightly strummed, and the melody played at [A] should be played fingerstyle – the combination works well.

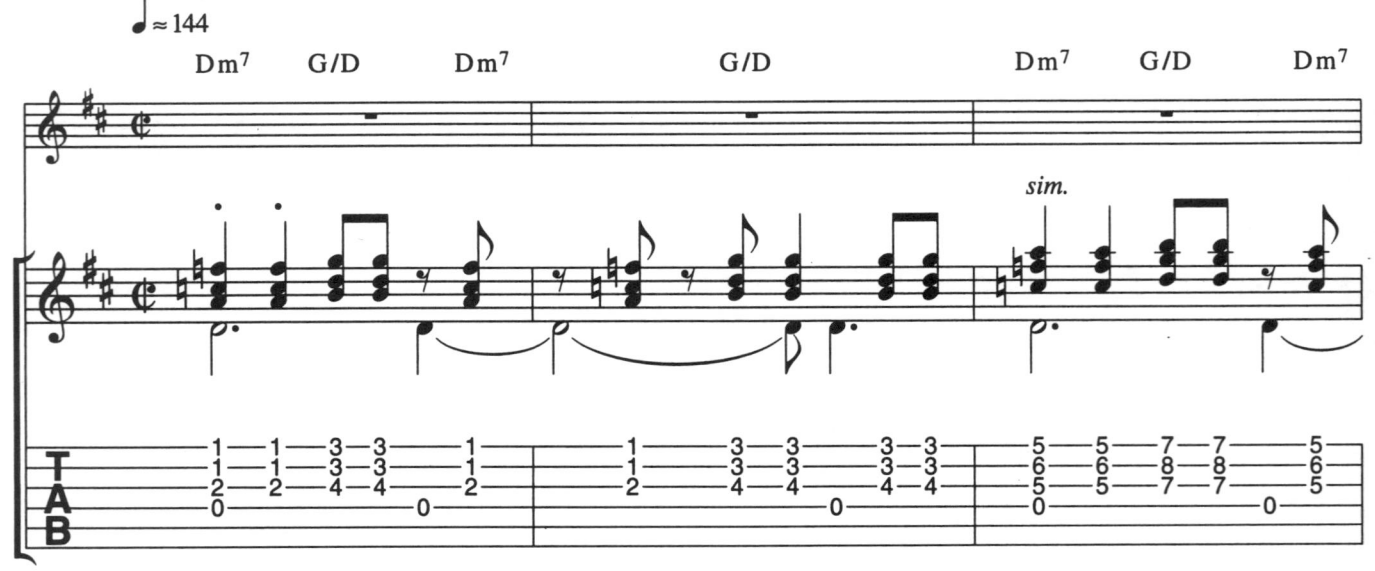

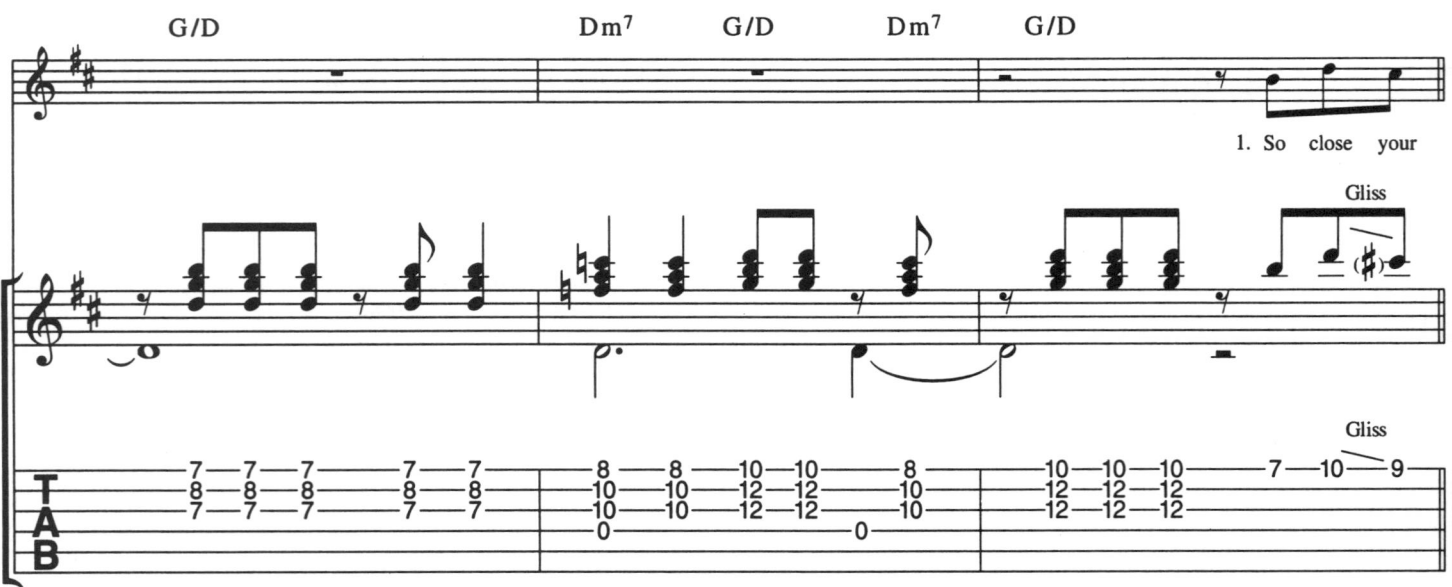

© copyright 1967 & 1976 corcovado music incorporated, usa
assigned to westminster music limited, suite 2.07, plaza 535 kings road, london sw10 for the united kingdom and eire
all rights reserved
international copyright secured

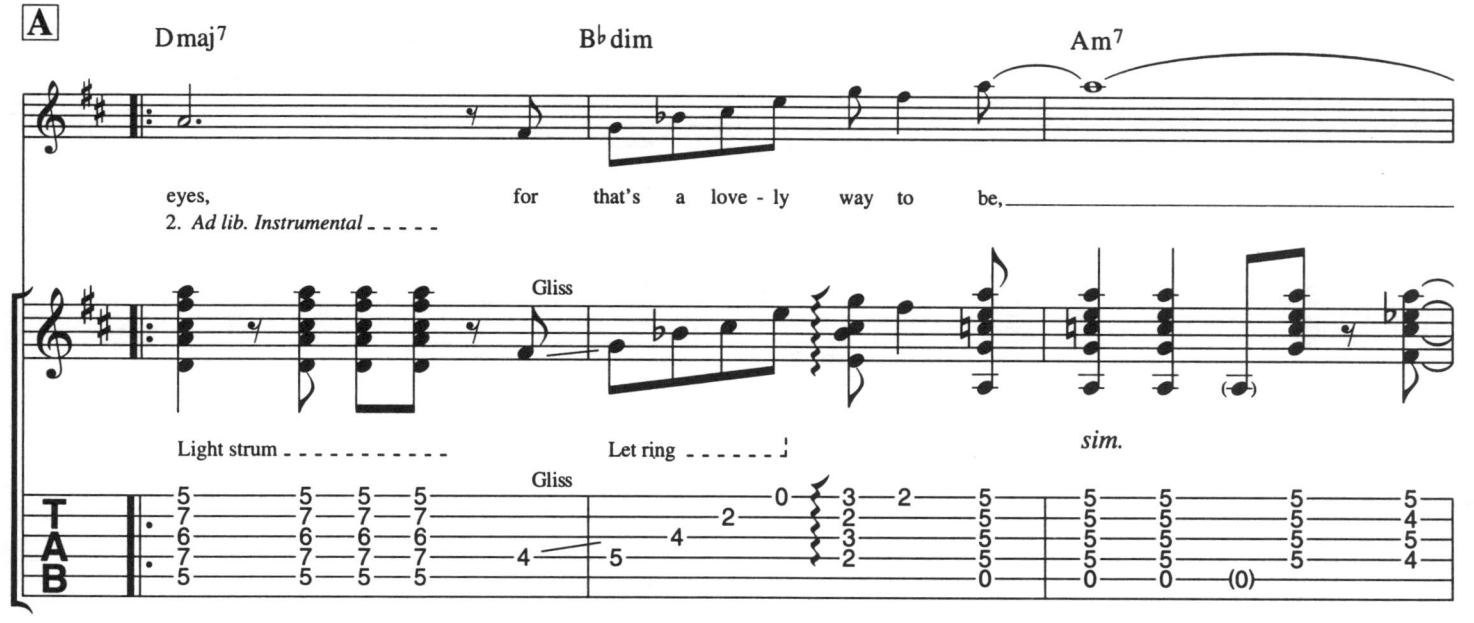

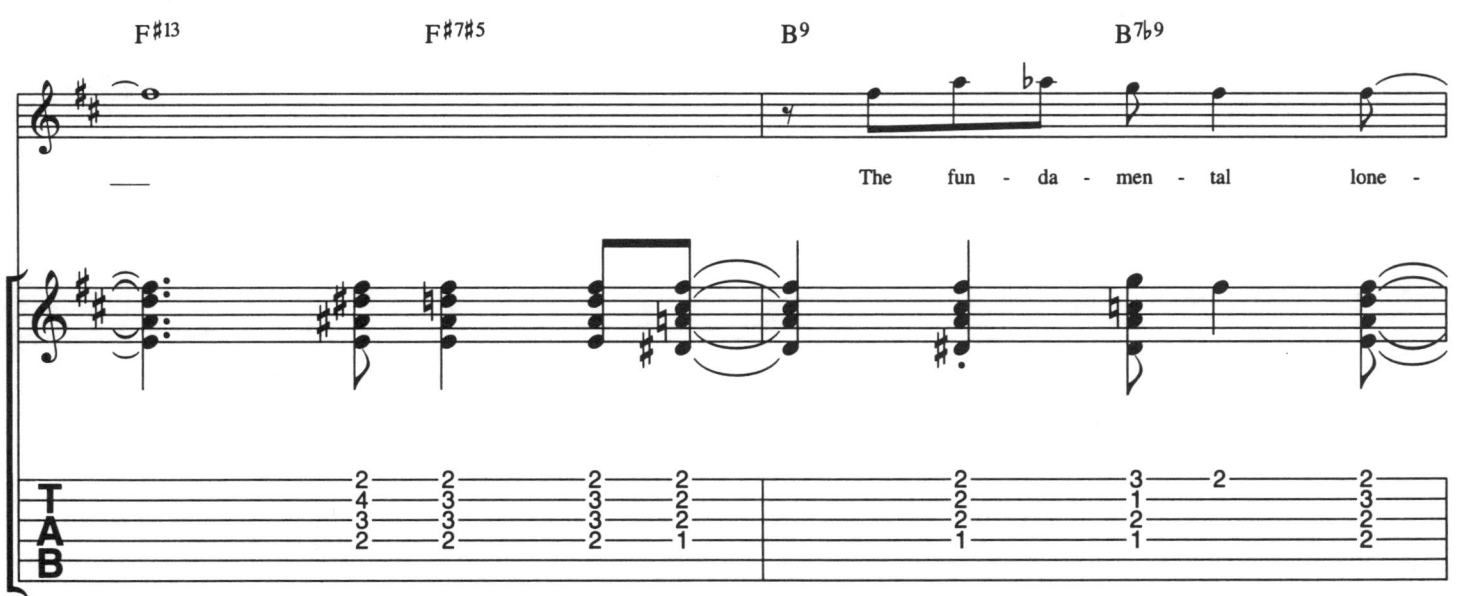

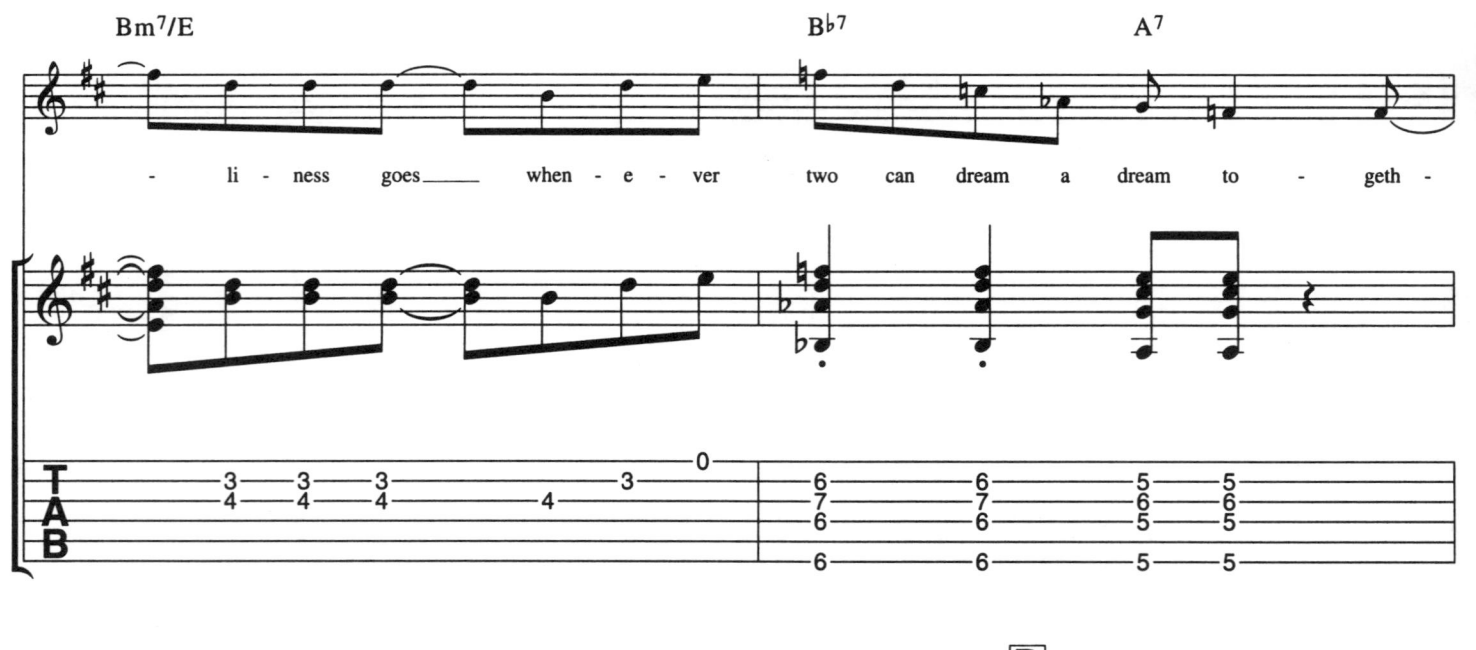
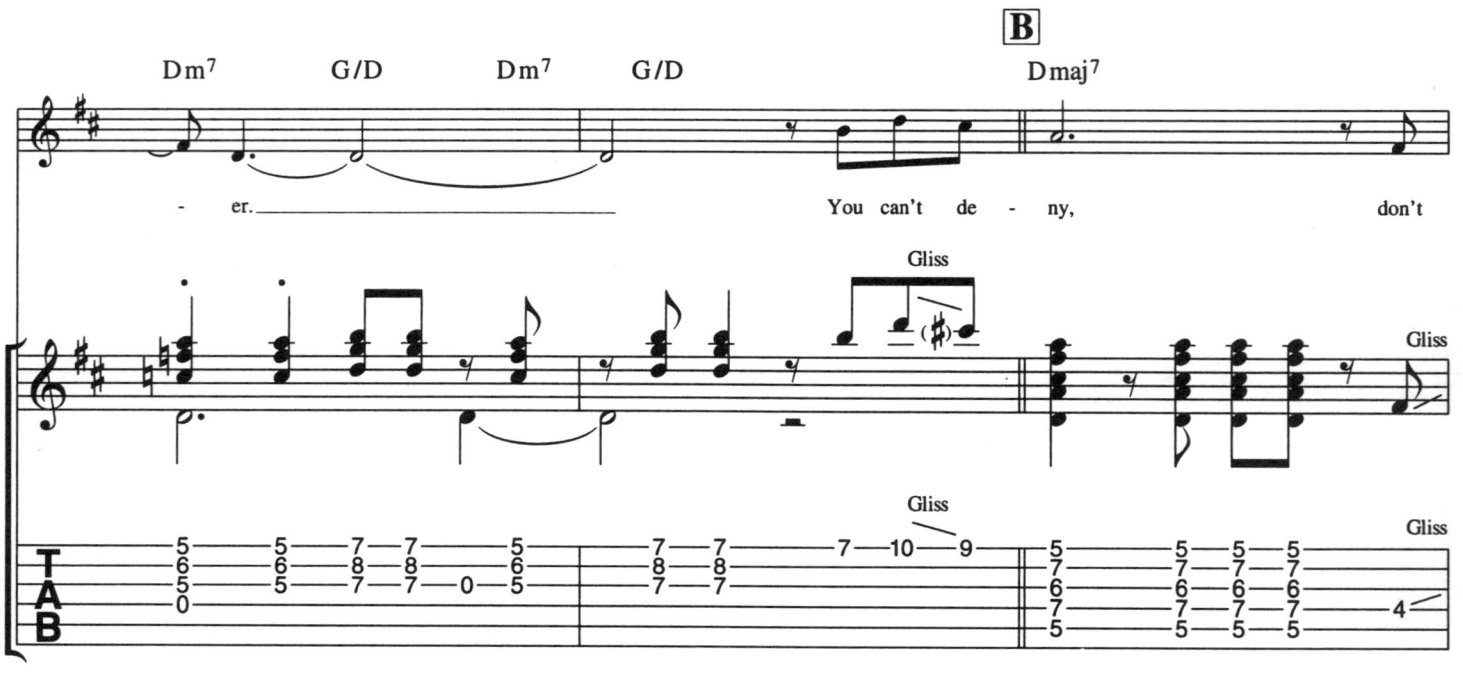
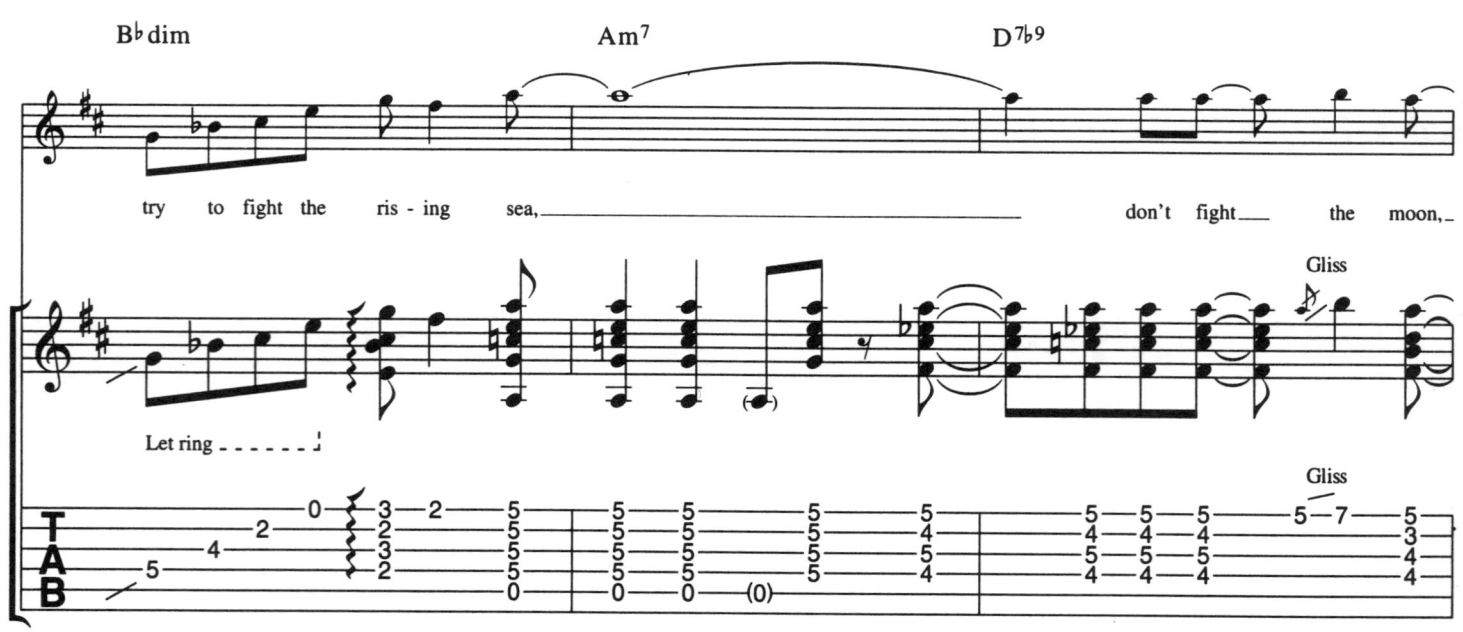

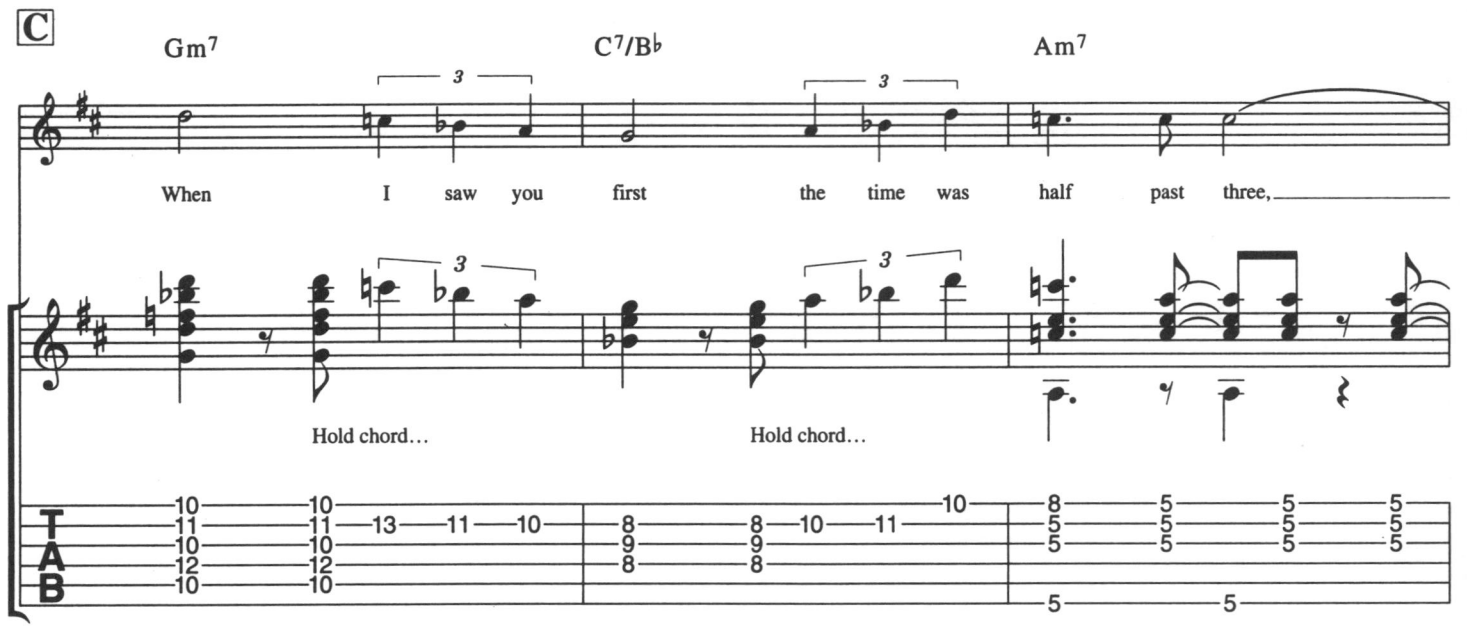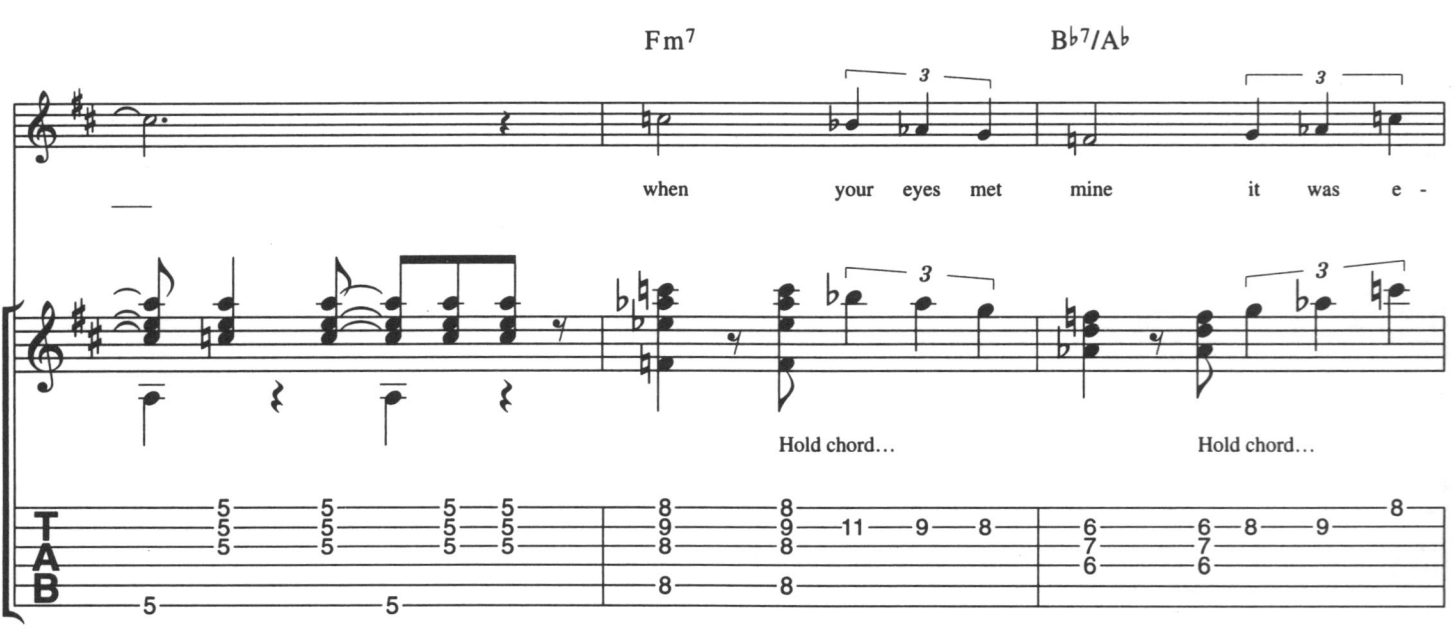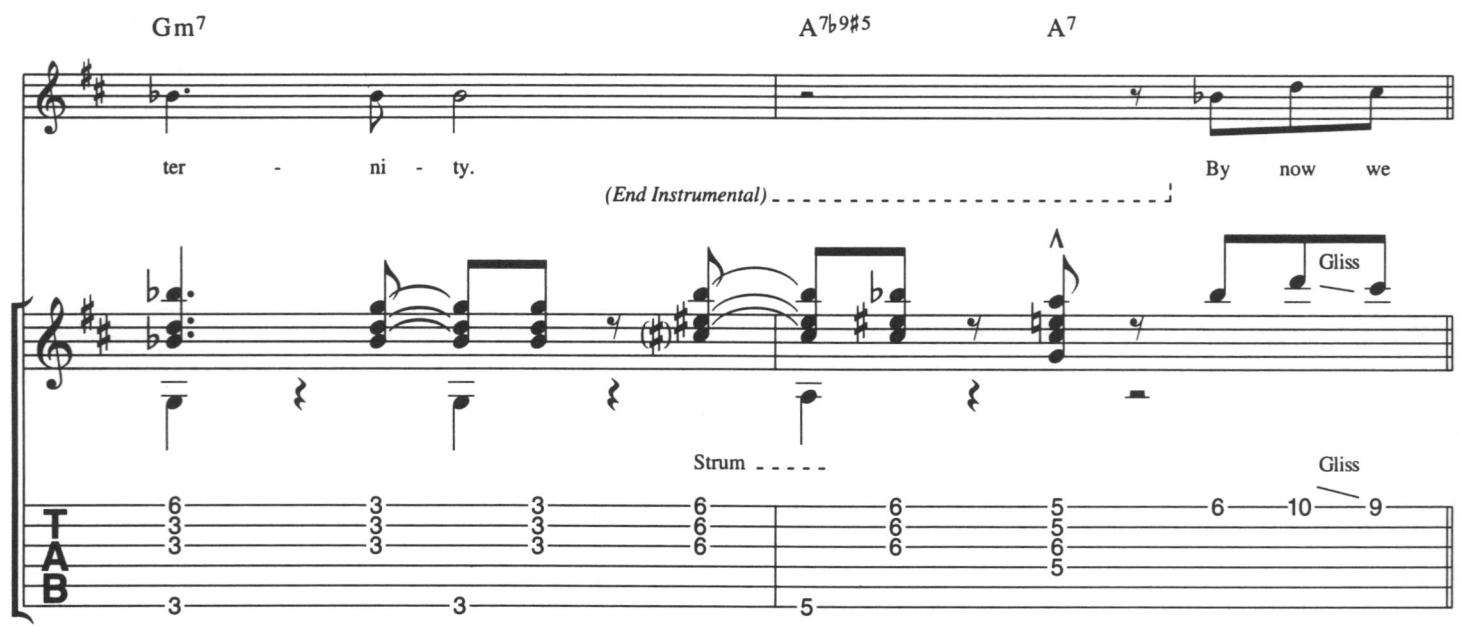

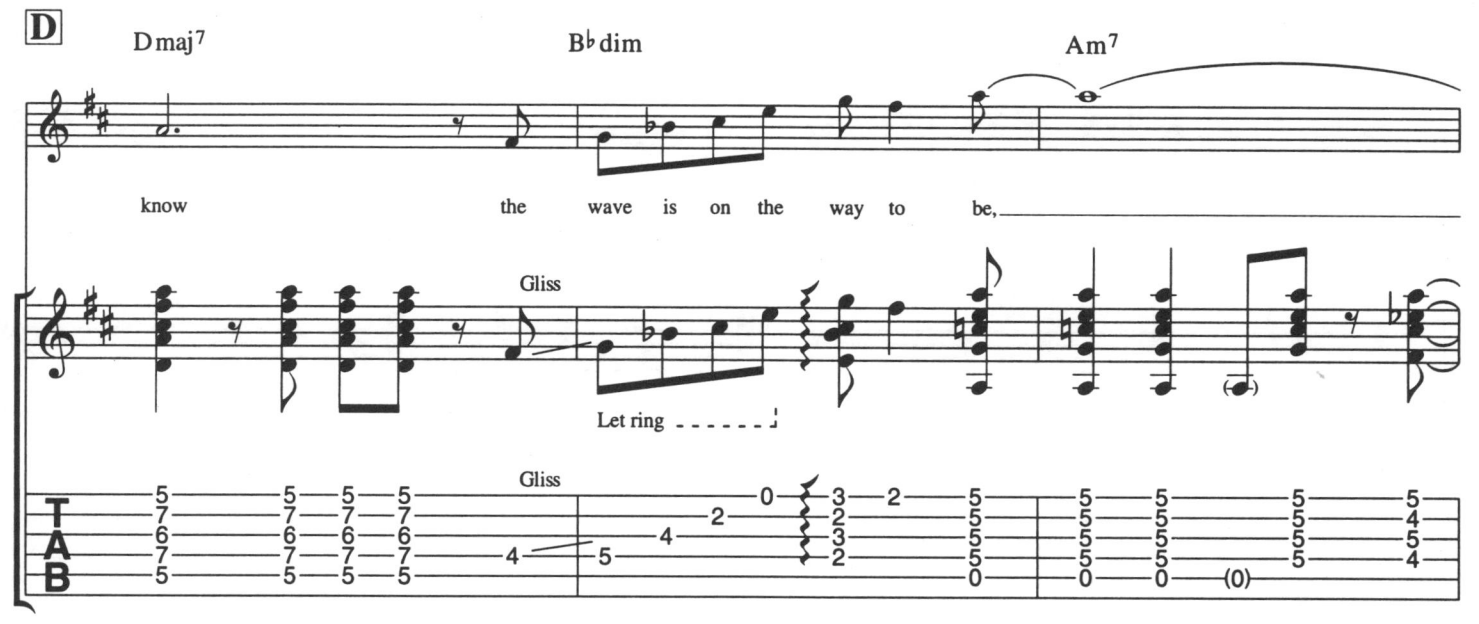
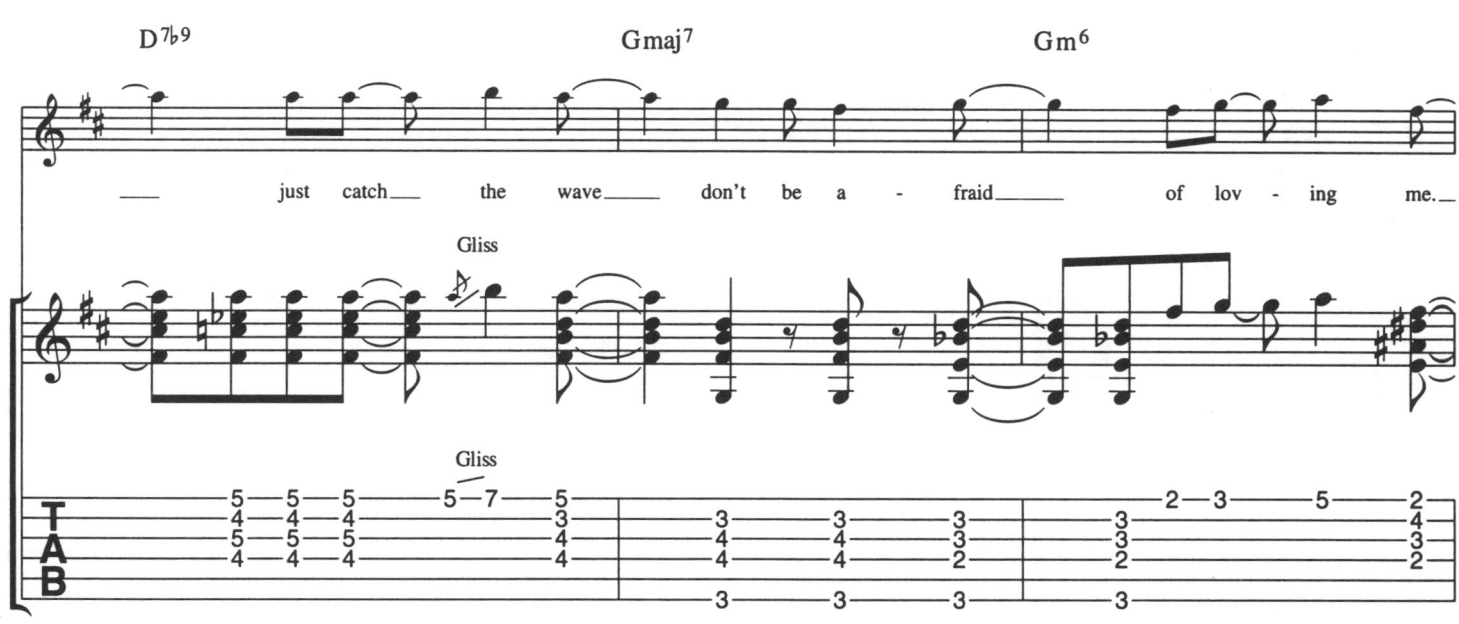
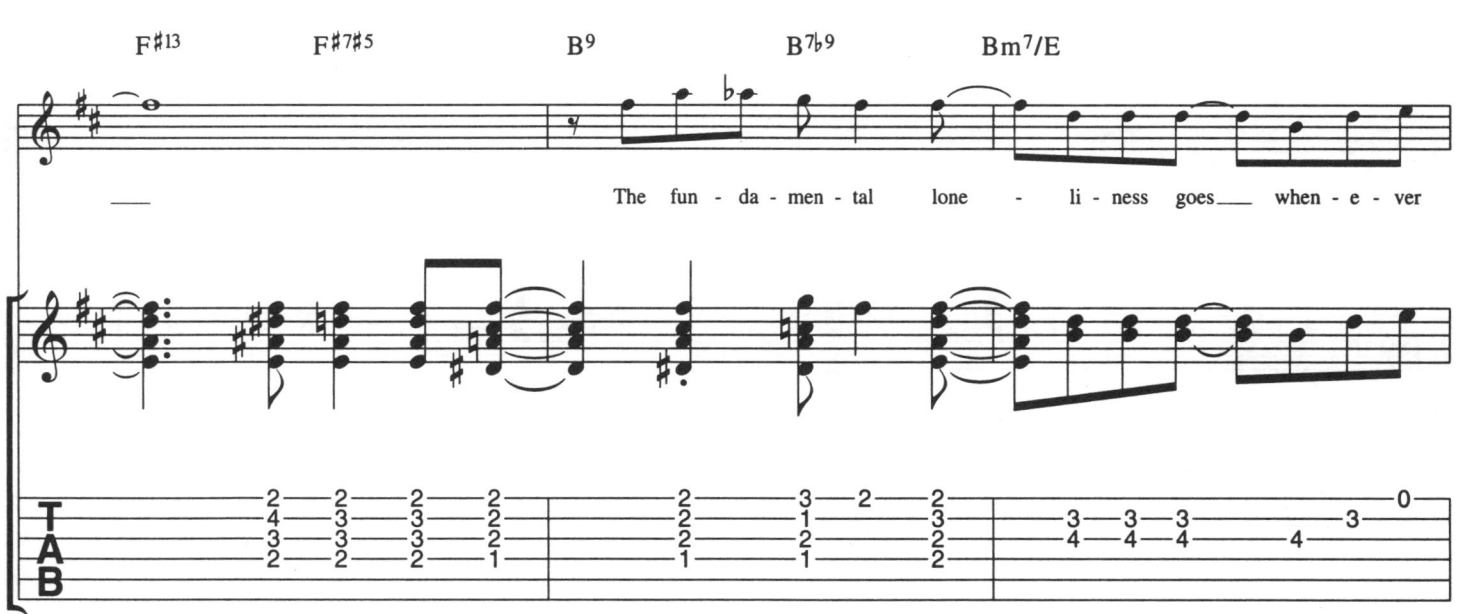